Lorenzo Dow McCabe

Divine nescience of future contingencies a necessity

Being an introduction

Lorenzo Dow McCabe

Divine nescience of future contingencies a necessity
Being an introduction

ISBN/EAN: 9783337221874

Printed in Europe, USA, Canada, Australia, Japan

Cover: Foto ©Andreas Hilbeck / pixelio.de

More available books at **www.hansebooks.com**

DIVINE NESCIENCE

OF

FUTURE CONTINGENCIES

A NECESSITY.

BEING AN INTRODUCTION TO "THE FOREKNOWLEDGE OF GOD, AND COGNATE THEMES."

By L. D. McCABE, D.D., LL.D.

"Persuasion is in Soul, Necessity is in Intellect."

NEW YORK:
PUBLISHED BY PHILLIPS & HUNT,
FOR THE AUTHOR.
1882.

Copyright 1882, by

L. D. McCABE,
Ohio.

PREFATORY NOTE.

"BUY the truth, and sell it not," is the voice of inspiration. Prov. xxiii, 23. Truth is very costly; it costs labor, patience, persistency, popularity, and multitudes of prejudices. But it ought to be bought at any price, and sold at no price. "I came into the world to bear witness to the truth," said the Redeemer. How sacred a thing must the truth be, if such a messenger should come from such a place, through such a distance, over such difficulties, down to such a world, to be its unchallenged witness.

I wish now to prove this proposition: Divine Nescience of Future Contingencies is a Necessity.

INTRODUCTION.

Professor L. D. M'Cabe, LL.D.—

My Esteemed Friend: I thank you for the opportunity you gave me of reading the manuscript of your new work on the "Divine Nescience," and I desire to express to you the deep interest and pleasure with which I studied it, and I am glad to be able also to say that I received from it much spiritual profit.

The Infinite One is so great and his perfections so unsearchable, and yet his relations to us so profound and far-reaching, that every attempt made in a reverent spirit, and with a candid desire to know more of his nature, and to understand better his relations to us, ought to be received with the same reverent spirit and the same candid inquiry. Such an investigation, too, though it may even fail of the whole truth, ought to be of moral and spiritual benefit to both the author and the reader. With such a spirit I feel assured you have pursued these studies, and with such a spirit I trust the public will read the result of your inquiries.

No one can doubt the sincere honesty with which

you have sought for the truth in regard to these profound questions, and every student must feel the weight of your profound thought, exact logic and clearness of statement. But when one is led by his investigations into a line of thought and to conclusions different from those which have obtained in general belief, he must expect to enter upon a field of battle. The world—even the learned world—no more readily receives new doctrines, or new forms of doctrine, now, than in the ages when men suffered martyrdom for their faith, and the world exacted it of them. The happy advance made in this respect in our day is, that the martyrdom is intellectual, and no longer by fire or the sword.

It is not easy to convine men of a truth that differs from commonly-received doctrine, and even when convinced of the new truth, the world is still slow to give up the old. That you advocate a view of the Divine foreknowledge essentially different from that which has been most widely held by all schools, of course you know, and that the *onus probandi* rests upon you. A belief in a certain mode of statement of these recondite elements in the divine nature, however old or however nearly unanimous, does not of itself determine the truth of such statement, but it creates so strong a presumption in its favor, and gives it such intrenchment in the accepted knowledge and faith of the world, that he who would change it challenges a great battle which will long and earnestly wage about him, even if the truth is on his side.

Of course, no one will claim that we have yet found out all about God, and I take it the field into which you have entered is a legitimate one for fresh and candid inquiry. Certainly there are difficulties still remaining, profound and far-reaching, in these higher, and, perhaps I should say, speculative realms of theology, which no present theory of belief has yet been able to solve. Neither Calvinism or necessity on the one hand, nor Arminianism and liberty on the other, solves all difficulties, nor can a solution be found in an eclecticism which would combine parts of both. It is certain a much nearer approach to a satisfactory theology has been made by Arminianism by discarding the theory of the eternal decrees and its logically-consequent doctrines of election, reprobation, and necessity; but it is equally certain that Arminianism has not freed us from all difficulties, and especially from those very serious embarrassments which you have so ably discussed, growing out of the doctrine of the divine foreknowledge of contingent or volitional events.

All thinkers have felt these embarrassments, and most have been compelled to hold them in abeyance as unsearchable things in the depths of the divine Being. Certainly no one should complain that you are willing to search in these depths, and out of your thought to offer to the world what seems to you the promise of a still nearer approach to a satisfactory solution of these questions than even Arminianism offers. It is certain that it is difficult, perhaps I should say impossible, for the intellect to conceive the possibility of even the divine Mind foreknowing events that are wholly dependent on what shall be the free choices of free beings. It is also difficult to see the difference, in real and practical fact, between the certainty of a divinely foreknown event and the necessity of it, and to clear such a certainly foreknown event from the same embarrassments as would arise from its necessity. But there is difficulty also, and perhaps greater, in conceiving of God as not being able to foreknow even a contingent event; or, in other words, to think of God as ignorant of or unknowing the future doings of his free beings. From the former difficulties we may be forced to take refuge in our inability to comprehend them; but from the latter difficulty there has been an instinctive tendency in all ages to recoil. True, this tendency may be the result of the world's habit for ages of assuming that God does know and foreknow all things, even the future actions of free beings, and does not of itself prove it to be so, leaving it a legitimate field for you to show if possible that it is not so.

That your argument is strong, profound, clear, and courageous, every candid reader will admit. Whether it is conclusive or not will be settled by the large, and, I trust, fair criticism which your book will evoke.

Your able argument, I think, clearly leads to this conclusion at least, that while with regard to the difficulties of Calvinism, or the theory of necessity, you are able to show, and in a very masterly manner do show, that "these things cannot be," with regard to Arminianism, or the theory of liberty, you are only able to show that we are not able to comprehend "how these things can be." This shows the immense advantage gained by Arminianism over Calvinism by eliminating the divine fore-ordination. It is possible, as you show in your argument, to gain many other points by eliminating also the divine foreknowledge of contingent events; but whether by thus clearing or relieving some difficulties, it does not create others as serious or more so, must be left to the just criticism which competent scholars will give to your book.

I would not attempt to express in this short letter any criticism favorable or unfavorable of your theory, but do desire to convey to you my high appreciation of the learning, scholarship and patient industry exhibited in your work. I rejoice that you have been able and willing to write this book, and hope you will soon give it to the public,

CONTENTS.

	PAGE
INTRODUCTION.	5

CHAPTER I.
DIVINE NESCIENCE OF FUTURE CONTINGENCIES IS A NECESSITY, IN THE NECESSITIES OF THINGS... 15

CHAPTER II.
DIVINE NESCIENCE OF FUTURE CONTINGENCIES IS A NECESSITY, IN THE NATURE OF THINGS... 32

CHAPTER III.
DIVINE NESCIENCE OF FUTURE CONTINGENCIES IS A NECESSITY, IN ORDER TO ESCAPE THE DREADED SYSTEM OF NECESSITY... 42

CHAPTER IV.
DIVINE NESCIENCE OF FUTURE CONTINGENCIES IS NECESSARY TO THE DIVINE PERFECTIONS... 44

CHAPTER V.
NESCIENCE OF FUTURE CONTINGENCIES IS NECESSARY TO SAFEGUARD THE WISDOM AND CANDOR OF THE HOLY GHOST... 62

CHAPTER VI.

DIVINE NESCIENCE OF FUTURE CONTINGENCIES IS A NECESSITY, TO ESCAPE THE CRUSHING SYSTEM OF PANTHEISM.. 65

CHAPTER VII.

DIVINE NESCIENCE OF FUTURE CONTINGENCIES IS NECESSARY TO GIVE VALIDITY TO OUR HOPES AND FEARS.... 69

CHAPTER VIII.

DIVINE NESCIENCE OF FUTURE CONTINGENCIES IS NECESSARY TO THE IMPRESSION THAT OUGHT TO BE MADE ON THE MIND OF A PROBATIONER FOR ETERNITY........... 72

CHAPTER IX.

DIVINE NESCIENCE OF FUTURE CONTINGENCIES IS NECESSARY TO AN INTERPRETATION OF THE HOLY SCRIPTURES. 75

CHAPTER X.

DIVINE NESCIENCE OF FUTURE CONTINGENCIES IS A NECESSITY, TO AN EXPLANATION OF THE UTILITY OF PRAYER.. 96

CHAPTER XI.

DIVINE NESCIENCE OF FUTURE CONTINGENCIES IS NECESSARY TO THE CONSTRUCTION OF A SATISFACTORY THEODICY. 101

CHAPTER XII.

DIVINE NESCIENCE OF FUTURE CONTINGENCIES IS NECESSARY TO A UNIVERSAL ATONEMENT 107

CHAPTER XIII.

Divine Nescience of Future Contingencies is a Necessity, for the Logical and Final Settlement of the Doctrine of Endless Punishment...................... 114

CHAPTER XIV.

Divine Nescience of Future Contingencies is Necessary to the Harmonizing of the Calvinian and Arminian Schools of Theology 149

CHAPTER XV.

The Reality of Time makes Divine Nescience of Future Contingencies an Imperative Necessity........ 278

CHAPTER XVI.

Concluding Observations............................ 290

DIVINE NESCIENCE

OF

FUTURE CONTINGENCIES A NECESSITY.

CHAPTER I.

DIVINE NESCIENCE IS A NECESSITY IN THE NECESSITIES OF THINGS.

NECESSARILY there must be a universe of necessities. The infinite uncaused Intelligence, time, space, mathematical truths, and, doubtless, innumerable other things unknown to us, must exist of necessity. They must exist, too, as necessary realities, not as necessary evolutions. Without the unquestioned assumption of the infinite Intelligence, any philosophy is simply impossible. Philosophy is the sphere of the knowable. If the infinite One, in all his activities and faculties, is under the reign of necessity, then there can exist but a single universe, the universe of necessities. But if he possess the attribute of freedom, and can act under the law of liberty, then there must be a second universe, the universe of contingencies. Contingent things are things that might be or might not be, that might come to pass or might not come to pass. If freedom is an attribute of the infinite One, a world of contingencies is logically inevitable. If he is free he cannot be controlled by modes, theories, uniformities, or idealities, in the exercise of his originative conceptions and creative energies. The moment you bind him with universal necessities you annihilate his freedom.

It is true that many specific necessities must be implied in and introduced into a universe of contingencies. These necessities enter as truths, principles, axioms, laws, limitations, possibles and impossibles. These fundamental necessities can neither be violated nor overlooked by the Creator in his works of creation. For his material creations he requires necessary truths and immovable foundations. In his construction of the solar system, for example, he did not violate any law of geometry or of numbers, quantity or mechanics. In his government of moral creatures he requires immutable moral distinctions, such as right, justice, equity and holiness, as objective inflexible standards of final appeal. To these inflexible standards he voluntarily conforms himself, and by them he is justified and vindicated in his moral administration before the moral universe.

Then, too, the infinite Thinker must be limited by many subjective necessities, some of which we know, but, doubtless, vastly more are unknown to us. Of these subjective necessities we may instance the necessary laws of thought, identity, self-contradiction, excluded middle and sufficient reason. These laws of thought constrain the Infinite as well as the finite logician. Noah Porter says: "The rational methods of the divine and human intellects must be the same, and induction is possible only on the assumption that the intellect of man is a reflex of the divine intellect." The laws of thought, therefore, must constrain the thought processes of the Infinite intellect.

And right here it is necessary that we carefully distinguish between an infinite being in the abstract and an infinite being in the concrete. An infinite being in the abstract is a bundle of infinities, bound up according to human conception or fancy. It would be more forcible, perhaps, to represent an infinite being in the abstract as a sphere of infinities, in which each infinity is insisting on itself, regardless of the claims of all other infinities. Infinite power, for example, may be conceived of as moving on regardless of the claims of infinite goodness, or as pressing on indifferent to infinite wisdom. Infinite mercy may be conceived of as bidding infinite justice and inflexible right to stand in abeyance and be silent. And the same conflict may be predicated of other attributes of an infinite being conceived of in the mere abstract. But to call such an abstract infinity, such a contradictory conception by the name of Deity, leads inevitably into incertitude and inextricable confusion. And it was conceiving of God as an infinity in the abstract that led the great Augustine into such erroneous and dangerous conceptions of the divine nature. The Augustinian conception of Deity was that of a universal infinite, that is, of a being infinite in all respects, and unlimited in all his attributes. But if God be infinite in every respect, he can neither be qualified nor conditioned in any respect. And if he cannot be qualified nor conditioned in any respect, he cannot be related; he cannot be a Creator, or a Father, or a Revealer, or an object of love, or a hearer of prayer, or a receiver of adoring worship. For who could worship a power too capricious to be limited by goodness? The distinguishing claims of the Augustinian theology are in reference to its logical consistency. But the very moment Augustinian theology completes its own logical processes it turns flatly against itself, and commits suicide. It is regretfully pronounced a veritable "*felo-de-se*" by myriads rigidly reared in the belief of its dogmas. Attributing to God the mathematical or metaphysical idea of infinity logically annihilates him in his concrete personality. And yet this Augustinian conception of God has fastened itself upon nearly all modern theology. This will amply explain the alarming tendencies of our age to scientific atheism, to materialism, to Unitarianism, and to a religious nihilism. It would be difficult for the widely-observant and patiently thoughtful upon theological themes to avoid this conviction in their moments of candor. The only possible escape for scriptural theology is in the denial that God is the Infinite in the abstract, possessing all infinities in the pure abstract, wholly unrestrained and unlimited, or that he is the universally infinite. I presume it was this contradictory conception of the infinite One that so puzzled and disheartened Hamilton and Mansel as to the possibility of our knowing him at all. Failure to discriminate between being in the abstract and being in the concrete would necessitate innumerable difficulties on that vital and momentous subject of knowing God. But our glorious God is not this infinity in the abstract. He is the infinite One in the concrete. The infinite power of God must be held in perfect control by infinite wisdom and goodness. His infinite mercy must revere law, justice, right, holiness and universal order. It is only within their *sanctum sanctorum* that mercy can ever be permitted to exercise its tenderness toward the unworthy.

All God's infinite attributes move on in ineffably harmonious relations from everlasting unto everlasting. This ineffable harmony that ever sounds throughout the universe in enrapturing strains is the result of the checks, control, limitations, mutabilities, and subjectivities, indispensable to a concrete, free infinite personality. His will holds each attribute in subserviency to the perfection and consistent activities of the whole. In this process are secured the glory of the divine character, and the well-being of his created, related, intelligent and accountable millions.

Besides all such necessary limitations in Deity, growing out of the divine personality, and the deep necessities of things, it would be a limitation seriously detrimental to infinite perfection to deny to him the glorious prerogative of self-denial, of limiting himself in his works of creation, according to his own freedom and the innumerable plans that freedom may originate. The perfection of an ideal universe requires the divine prerogative of creating a free-will, that can in the exercise of its freedom resist and withstand Omnipotence, and the infinite Will. And freedom, in such a creature, would necessitate specific, modified mutabilities and limitations in the experiences and activities of the Creator. These mutabilities, for reasons best known to himself, he freely imposes upon himself. If we would think of the infinite One, to any valuable philosophical result, we must think of him as restrained and constrained by such perfecting necessities, and submitting himself to such modified mutabilities.

In the realm of necessities God can have no new thoughts, desires, purposes or plans. But freedom in an infinite being implies that contingent things may certainly be brought into existence. In the realms of the contingent, should such a realm be resolved upon, he must necessarily have new thoughts, new desires, purposes and plans. Freedom implies origination, and origination implies bringing from nonentity something into existence. A thing that might or might not have an existence, if it actually have an existence, that existence must have a beginning. If the conception of a thing existed in the divine mind from eternity, then that conception could not have been the creation of his free volition. If it was not the creation of his free volition it was a necessity, and no contingency at all, and

God had no agency whatever in its creation or in its origination. A contingent entity can have no possible beginning, save in an unconstrained volition. If the conception of a thing that does not exist existed from eternity, then the conceptions of all things that do not exist must have existed from eternity; but this is absurd. If the conception of a thing that does not exist is not eternal, then there must have been a time before it was conceived of. But if that conception had a beginning, it must have resulted from a free being, for it is not possible for an entity to emerge out of nonentity. If an uncaused cause produce an effect, it must do it without being constrained to do it; for no caused cause could possibly coerce an uncaused cause. Philosophy necessitates and the Bible every-where represents God as taking the absolute initiative. To deny him the power of initiation would be a limitation to his perfections from which we all would shrink. But this requires power to conceive of something that previously had not existence. If God has power to initiate, he has power to precede initiation by original thinking. This power of original thinking he must begin to exercise at some point in infinite duration. For if he never did begin to exercise this power of original thinking, we have no evidence that he ever could think originally, or that he ever could conceive of a single new conception. If he has no power to originate new conceptions, he is a necessary being. Our conceptions of him would at once congeal into the iceberg of fatality.

Initiatives necessarily involve and imply freedom, and freedom logically necessitates contingencies; but divine revelation as well as freedom requires the existence of things purely contingent. If God is a free being he must have an arena for the exercise of his liberty. His power of self-determination must be the profoundest and brightest of all the faculties of his incomprehensible nature. Such an arena he found in creating worlds, and in endowing them with qualities, forces, missions, and adornments, pleasant for himself to behold, and highly illustrative of his mental, moral, and governmental perfections. But with this wide and magnificent arena he was not completely satisfied; he, therefore, created free moral agents, immortal souls in his own image and likeness, co-creators, co-causes, co-originators, and co-eternal with himself in the realms of the contingent.

Then arose before him the new and most interesting arena for the exercise of the divine freedom in the free untrammeled determinations of accountable beings made in his own likeness. In the creation of beautiful, but irresponsible things, and in the moral government of responsible agents, the divine freedom had a theater for its activity, inexpressibly entertaining to the divine mind, and enrapturing to the divine heart.

The divine freedom rejoices over the existence of basal necessities, but it stands upon the frontier of the realms of the contingent, peering into their fathomless possibilities. Through the boundless realms of the may or may not be, divine freedom ranges far and wide, to find that on which, with profit to the universe and gratification to itself, it may exert its exhaustless activities. The eternity to come will unfold contingencies which are not and cannot now be in the divine consciousness. Such possibilities are necessary to the perfection of God, considered relative to his historical and continuous life in the objective, and also relative to the essential activities of an infinite mind.

God possesses the power, therefore, of awakening original thoughts and taking the initiative, as he may sovereignly determine, in the untrammeled exercise of his absolute freedom. This possibility of unthought-of contingencies yet to come will keep the intelligent universe, throughout eternity, in endless expectancies of new unfoldings of God's infinite resources to instruct, expand, elevate and entertain beings created in his own intellectual and moral image. This view of Deity invests his glorious character with perfections utterly impossible under any theory of absolute prescience, or of unconditional predestination.

But the Scriptures represent *man* as having also the power of taking the absolute initiative. If he is not a free being there can be for him neither right, wrong, justice, injustice, moral philosophy, or moral government. If he is not free, then conscience, remorse, and the "certain fearful looking for of judgment and fiery indignation, which shall devour the adversaries" of God, are all false, and are really most inexcusable phantoms.

While to necessary things there is necessarily no beginning, to contingent things there necessarily must be a beginning; that beginning cannot possibly reflect any thing back into its anterior. If it does, then it is not an absolute beginning. A contingent thing must be a pure origination by a being possessing power to select and originate one out of many. But this is possible only on the hypothesis that the future is now undetermined, unfixed, and, therefore, uncertain in the universe of contingencies.

Omniscience is "the power of knowing all things," says Worcester. God knows all things that now exist, that have ever existed, that will ever exist, as the result of existing causes acting in the lines of cause and effect, and all that he has determined to bring into existence. For his omniscience he has grounds of knowledge perfectly valid. As to pure contingencies prior to their creation he may have theories, ideals, fancies, possibilities or probabilities, but cannot have certain knowledge. Relative to them there is absolutely nothing that is knowable. "If there could be contingencies it would be impossible for God to foreknow them," is the uniform testimony of all leading Calvinians. "Without decree," says Jonathan Edwards, "foreknowledge could not exist." "There can be no certainty that does not depend upon the divine purpose," says Dr. Hodge. They all concede the incapacity of Omniscience to foreknow the certain existence of a thing that might or might not be, a thing that might or might not come to pass. Of contingencies, we affirm, God can have no knowledge until from the realm of the possible a free being originates their conception and determines to actualize those conceptions into entities. It is only from that moment that a contingency becomes a knowable thing. Up to the point of some free being originating its conception and determining to actualize it, it is a pure unreality. Between the earth and the moon there might or might not exist a second satellite. Such a world is now an unreality, and hence it is a thing that is unknowable; and if it is a thing unknowable, it is no reflection upon Omniscience to affirm its incapacity to know it. On the morrow the Creator might conceive and determine to make such an addition to the solar system. Then it would be a reality, and, therefore, it would be knowable. Even the conception of a future contingency that may be brought into existence by man as an actuality has no present existence in any mind, finite or infinite. The only conceivable cause of a contingency is a free will, and a will to be free can have no coercing or determining antecedents, moral or material.

And here we must distinguish between the intelligence of Deity and his intellectuality. His intellectuality, his capacity to know, is perfect, without any deficiency or weakness; it is an element of his necessary existence, and, therefore, is wholly subjective. But his intelligence is the knowing, and is the result of the exercise of his intellectuality. Intelligence is derived from intuition, from consciousness, from inference, and from observation. Intelligence derived from intuition and necessary consciousness can never be increased or decreased.

Intelligence derived from inference and observation must be derived from objectivity, but objectivity is the realm of the contingent. Intelligence of the contingent can never exist until the contingencies exist, because a nonentity can have no objectivity. That which is a present conceivable nonentity may become an actual entity. But the apprehension of a possible entity is theory, but not knowledge. We must distinguish between the intelligence of entities and the apprehension of possibles, between God's consciousness of necessary existences, and his intelligence derived from his inference and from his observation of unnecessitated things.

Failing to make this discrimination, men infer that God's intelligence of contingencies is just as immutable as his intelligence of necessities. In the realm of necessities all God's thoughts are immutable from everlasting to everlasting; but in the realm of contingencies he can at pleasure will worlds into existence. If he will new worlds into being he can will new conceptions, new plans, new enterprises into existence. Having the power to will new thoughts into existence, he has the power to originate new creations, new purposes for the glorification of his intelligent creatures, for the adornment of his material universe and the illustration of his own glorious perfections. His consciousness derived from necessities must be different from his consciousness derived from actual contingencies.

In these views of the divine nature I am gratified in being supported by Dr. Dorner, of the University of Berlin, one who stands in the foremost rank of living Protestant divines. In a recent number of the *Bibliotheca Sacra* he says: " Any view of the divine nature that excludes all distinction, movement and change from God is incompatible with the idea of creation. The world, as a thought, was a determination given to his mind by God. He must have conceived the world as changeable, or he would not have willed it thus to be. In the divine omniscience there must be an element of growth. If there be free beings there must be free determinations. God may have a prior knowledge of them as mere possibilities, but he cannot have a knowledge of them as actualities. This knowledge of human acts must be acquired gradually as they come to pass. This knowledge he draws from history, and it is conditioned by the action of the causalities which he has brought into existence. In his counsels, in his knowledge and in his volitions with respect to the world, in his relations to time and space, God is not unchangeable. In these regards he undergoes movement and change, and suffers himself to be conditioned." Six months after I had published a work on the Divine Foreknowledge I found, with inexpressible pleasure, these and kindred thoughts from the pen of the great historian of Protestant theology.

Now, if man has the power of taking the absolute initiative, he can, through grace, bring himself into conscious union with his Creator, or he can make himself an incorrigible outcast. He can, through faith and prayer, bring countless blessings upon his fellows, or, through iniquity, he can bring upon them unnumbered curses. If these diverse classes of possibilities are before him awaiting his selection, then the future must now be undetermined and uncertain, as his unoriginated initiations are now uncertain. A future that is now fixed and infallibly certain could not present an appropriate arena for such unoriginated, uncoerced, unimplied and undetermined initiations. The only proper future for such undetermined initiations must be one that is now unfixed, undetermined, and, therefore, uncertain. If man can achieve rewardability or bring substantial blessings and effect far-reaching changes upon the human family, then the future must be undetermined and remain undetermined until he, by his free, self-originating will, will determine it.

If man can of himself form an original conception of a thing, if he can at will bring or not bring that thing from nonentity into the universe of contingent entities, and if in willing it into existence he exercises an element of power that is wholly other than and apart from that of his Creator, then the provision of such initiatives must be an utter impossibility. If he cannot do those things, he cannot be an originator of moral character. In making man a free being, capable of originating volitions, God was compelled in the deep necessities of things to leave his future unsettled, unfixed, and unknown. And in making man such a being, he bound upon himself the solemn obligation of varying his treatment of him in the way of rewards and punishments, smiles and frowns, in exact accordance with his self-originated volitions. Freedom in the creature necessitates this modified mutability in the Creator.

"In the world," says Dr. Dorner, "God must live an historical life, a life that is conditioned by man's use of freedom. For neither Omnipotence nor divine love holds undivided sway over man. His freedom is a co-operative factor, and his own acts condition both the operations and the communications of God. Neither intellect nor heart can be satisfied with a view of God which represents him as remaining eternally the same, for present, past, and future, instead of his position and feelings assuming a form correspondent to man's character." These earnest thoughts of the great thinker cannot lightly be set aside by the logical inquirer. Dr. Dorner wrote me that he had read my book with great satisfaction and agreed with me in most of my propositions.

Morality, moral character, moral government, accountable beings, and the creation of the universe, all necessitate freedom in the Creator. Accountability, conscience, rewards and punishments, consciousness and likeness to his Maker, all necessitate untrammeled freedom in man. Freedom necessitates objective initiatives, and objective initiatives necessitate subjective incipiencies, and absolute incipiencies have their origin necessarily in the volition of a free-will, a will possessing the power of alternative choices.

These subjective incipiencies can have no existence, therefore, until they have been originated by a sovereign will, and hence they are unforeknowable. "Even God," said Dr. Jamison, a rigid Calvinian, "cannot know what his future choices will be until he has determined those choices." · Perfection of Deity necessitates his freedom, and his freedom necessitates incognizable things. "Deny contingency, and all in morals and religion worth contending for vanishes out of sight," said Dugald Stewart. "Better deny prescience than contingency," said Dr. Tappan in his review of Edwards. Philosophical thinking logically necessitates the existence of an infinite Being. The perfection of this infinite Intelligence necessitates his freedom. This freedom necessitates that the distinction between liberty and constraint should be as radical as the distinction between matter and mind, or the distinction between accountability and unaccountability, or that between spiritual powers and material forces. This radical distinction between liberty and constraint necessitates the absence of all analogies between them whether considered in themselves, or in the laws of their freedom, or in the products of their activities. Analogy between free volitions and constrained sequences is inconceivable. The absence of all analogies between constrained sequences and free volitions analogically necessitates that there be also a distinction in the mode of their prognosis. For when two subjects differ in every known particular, analogy requires that they should differ in a specified unknown particular. Therefore if constrained sequences require prescience, free volition must require nescience.

But freedom in an infinite Intelligence necessitates also contingencies. Contingencies are and must be instantaneous originations in the absence of all eternal conceptions thereof. Contingencies originate in no anterior causes, but are created by beings possessing the power of inception, and alternative choices necessitate present nescience of what may be the elective exercises of this alternative choosing power.

We thus see that the Divine nescience of future contingencies is a necessity grounded in the profoundest necessities of things, and hence cannot be regarded as an imperfection in the Deity. Prescience and originality are incompatible propositions. But to originality Divine nescience is absolutely indispensable.

CHAPTER II.

DIVINE NESCIENCE OF FUTURE CONTINGENCIES IS A NECESSITY IN THE NATURE OF THINGS.

BY the nature of things I mean the nature the Creator gave them and the relations he instituted between them. Unless there be some element of my nature that in its voluntary exercise is independent of Deity, morality or immorality is impossible. Morality implies power freely to volitionate concordantly or discordantly with the will of God. There is absolutely no other place on which to posit accountability.

Accountability must necessarily rest on the exercise of a power that in its exercise, taken in a governmental sense, is wholly independent of the wishes, volition and purposes of the supreme Ruler.

I know that I can originate moral or immoral acts, simply because I am an accountable being. I cannot be accountable unless I am just as free and just as capacitated to choose disobedience as I am to choose obedience. This is so axiomatic that it never would have been denied, save in the prepossession of a theological theory, which was regarded as necessary to a complete system of theology. But, if possible, I have a stronger proof that I am an absolute originator in the fact that I can freely originate *sin*, a thing which I know God hates perfectly, dreads equally, and cannot look upon with allowance. He has no use for it, for he regards it as the great disturber of the peace and welfare of his moral universe, the great disorganizer and defeater of his glorious purposes. It is amazing blasphemy to charge in the remotest manner or in the least degree upon Deity the origin of sin, that great enemy of all happiness, whether finite or infinite. The great mystery that has been thrown over the origin of sin is merely the result of undue theological assumptions and false theories. You can to-day choose or refuse to forge a note. If you choose to forge one, you do it freely and without constraint, as your conscience, your consciousness and your self-degradation all unmistakably attest. But if you do it you emphatically originate sin. If you sin when you are not necessitated to sin you originate sin, and whoever first originated sin originated it just as you did; and really there is no more mystery about the origin of sin, notwithstanding all the ponderous tomes written in its explication, than there is about any willful sin of your every-day life. But I will return to this point in subsequent polemics.

Reason, remorse, conscience, accountability and the moral government of God, all unmistakably fix the origin of sin in the human will, and not a single element, or filament, or fiber of it originated anywhere else. The simple and single choice of a free will was the absolute incipiency of moral evil into the moral universe. Prior to that choice sin had no inception. If I am an originator, my determination before I made it had no previous incipiency. If it had no previous incipiency, then its previous incipiency had no existence. It was a nonentity, and if it was a nonentity it was unknowable; for if one nonentity is knowable then all nonentities are knowable, and this would fill the infinite Mind with an infinite number of nonentities. But this is painfully absurd. For God can no more know all nothings than he can do all nothings. How absurd the doing of a nothing, but equally absurd is the knowing of a nonentity. Indeed, knowledge of a nothing is self-contradictory, and my free choice before I made it is a nothing. But a nothing, says Worcester, is a nonentity. Knowledge necessarily involves the certainty of that which is known. Being must be the correlate of knowledge.

"If the will of man be free," says Toplady, with a liberty *ad utrum libet*, "and if his actions be the offspring of his own will, such of his actions as are not yet wrought must be radically and eventually uncertain." "It is impossible," says Jonathan Edwards, "for a thing to be certainly foreknown to any intellect without evidence." But no understanding, created or uncreated, can see evidence where there is no evidence. But if there be a future event that is a contingent event, the future existence of that event is now absolutely without evidence, and, therefore, no such future event can be now certainly foreknown. "A free agent," says the elder Hodge, "has the liberty of acting or not acting. He possesses the power of performing an action different from the one he does eventually perform. Now, either there did exist a reason why one action took place and not the other, or no such reason existed. If no such reason existed why one action took place and not the other, then all knowledge of the action before it occurred is necessarily excluded. For a knowledge of it would be to suppose knowledge without the least foundation of that knowledge in the object. God cannot know that something exists when nothing exists. If an event be certainly foreknown it must have a certain future existence, and for it there must be some reason or cause. Now that cause is either the purpose of God or it is something else. If that cause is the purpose of God, then the event is decreed. If it be some other cause, whatever that may be, as it fixes the certainty of the event, it must be as inconsistent with freedom as if the same effect were produced by the divine purpose."

Now I affirm that in both of these positions Dr. Hodge is right. For the reason or the cause why one act and not the other takes place must be something brought to bear upon the will from without. If we locate the incipiency of an act in something objective to the will, then something objective to the will constrains it as effectually as would the eternal decree of God. But if we locate the incipiency of an act in the pure will itself, and not in something objective to the will, then there is, without the least controversy, no possible sign or criterion or evidence to indicate what the future choice of the person will be.

"A free act," says Dr. L. P. Hickok, " hangs in perfect suspense. It comes with a touch, and a voluntary touch determines it." Now, I say, if a voluntary touch of a free-will determines the act, previously it must have been undetermined. No reason, motive or cause outside of the will can be the cause of the free choice of an accountable act. A free act is an absolute beginning, and cannot be represented by any factors previous to its occurrence. When we admit the existence of pre-existing factors or subtile influences or objective temptations to furnish evidence what the choice will be, we destroy the freedom of the will and break down our accountability.

True, there must necessarily be occasions for the will to act, and there must be opportunities for it to choose between alternate motives. These occasions are reasons, considerations addressed to the intellect, or motives addressed to the sensibilities. Without a soul and objects to be desired, and desires and reasons for acting, the will could not act. These are the general conditions of voluntary action. The intellect and the sensibilities being under the law of cause and effect, reasons and motives can act on the will only according to the same law, whereas the will acts under a law totally dissimilar. Few mental discriminations are more marked in their differences than the distinction between the action of the law of liberty and the action of the law of cause and effect. The action of the law of cause and effect is always shut up to a single result, while the action of the law of liberty is never shut up to a single result. The will may elect one or another or none of many alternates. In the action of the law of cause and effect the effect is always the measure of the cause and the cause is the measure of the effect; while in the action of the law of liberty the effect is seldom in proportion to the motive which is presented as the occasion of voluntary action. The action of the law of cause and effect can never achieve the least moral character, while the action of the law of liberty always creates moral character, and moral character is conceivable or possible under no other kind of action.

Things which are so unlike as the action of the law of liberty and the action of the law of cause and effect. ought surely to be expressed by terms suggestive of their nature and of their radical differences. The word *constraint* expresses the action of the law of cause and effect. But I know of no single word that expresses the action of the law of liberty. I, therefore, venture to make one, and call it *personic action*. Surely *personic* is a word as idiomatic as sermonic, and much more needed in the language. Any man has a right to make a new word, if it be needed, and the idiom is preserved, says Dr. Campbell. Personic action implies the power of alternative choices. Its voice is sovereign over all the occasions of volition, and autocratic in its action over all testing, proving, antecedents. A person is a being who can elect between competing reasons and conflicting motives, and then from original resolves.

And right here is the power of personic action to achieve moral worthiness. The great doctrine of justification by faith implies that in that work something is done by man which, as a condition, necessitates something to be done freely by God. This something done by God is necessitated by divine promise conditioned upon man's compliance with the required conditions of repentance and positive faith. This something done by man has necessarily its incipiency in human freedom. This human incipiency necessitates a divine incipiency. The human incipiency could have had no previous existence. The divine incipiency, therefore, could have had no possible anterior other than a pure uncertain contingency. Personic action being wholly sovereign and independent of constraining influences, there is nothing to indicate its final determination. To foreknow that determination is, therefore, knowing without any possible foundation for the knowledge. And to know without evidence is certainly absurd.

Still, the prescient freedomist may imagine that he has a way out of this difficulty in the fact that while God foresees the future free act, he sees also that the free agent will at the very time possess power to choose differently.

But this long-cherished and much-repeated fancy of the Arminian arises from his strangely confounding two propositions which are perfectly distinct. "It is now certain that I *will* choose life or death," is confounded with the proposition, "It is now certain that I *can* choose life or death."

"It is now certain that in the future I can choose life or death" is a proposition that expresses the present certainty that I shall be able or shall be capable of choosing either life or death in the future.

But this alternation refers to the theoretical question of human liberty, a purely speculative question of philosophy. But the alternation expressed in the proposition, "It is now certain that I *will* choose life or death," refers not to the speculative question of moral liberty, but to the practical question of the actual exercise of that faculty.

The former alternation refers to a theoretical doctrine, and has none but logical results in a thought system. But the alternation expressed in the proposition, "I will choose life or death," is a question of fact, a practical question of tremendous interest, and it is attended with everlasting results, delightful or dreadful. One alternation refers to the existence of the faculty of freedom, the other alternation refers to the actual exercise of that faculty.

If foreknowledge be true, there can be now no alternation as to the specific future exercise of my capability of freedom. If there be no alternation as to the future exercise of my faculty of freedom, then the proposition, "I will in the future choose life or death" is meaningless and very vexatious. The proposition is an absurdity if one of the two alternates is already certain: "I will in the future choose life;" "I will in the future choose death." If these propositions are not alternates, there is no ground of their alternation, and if there is no ground for their alternation, then the proposition "I will in the future choose life or death" is meaningless, and was framed only to deceive and mislead me.

For the certainty of one of two alternates destroys the alternation, and prevents the two alternates from being alternates. If there is ground for the alternation, the two events are alternates. But if they are alternates, each taken singly must necessarily be uncertain in itself. The present certainty that either A or B will take place is a very different certainty from the certainty that A and not B will take place. *John will go north* is a proposition that means something. It expresses a specific fact. *John will go north or east* means something. It means an alternation. It means that uncertainty attaches to both routes. The moment you give certainty to either of the routes you make the proposition *John will go north or east* meaningless and tantalizing. The only way you can give to this proposition any sense at all is to deny any present certainty to either of the directions. Foreknowledge renders this proposition nugatory and void of significance, by giving certainty to one of the two routes. Prescience, then, must unavoidably be rejected by every consistent and logical libertarian. A surrender of prescience is indispensable to the respectability of Arminianism. God must know things as they are, or his knowledge is unreliable. His knowing things as they are necessitates that he perceive the uncertainty as to which of two alternates will eventually come to pass or be determined. Alternation, in the nature of things, necessitates subjective uncertainty in the divine mind. The state of omniscience is, therefore, a state of uncertainty as to which of the alternates will certainly come to pass. And this snatches from the hand of the Arminian prescientist his long-cherished, fallacious fancy. But enough has been adduced to show that, in the nature of things as divinely constituted, divine nescience of future contingency is an unquestioned necessity.

CHAPTER III.

DIVINE NESCIENCE OF FUTURE CONTINGENCIES IS A NECESSITY IN ORDER TO ESCAPE THE DREADED SYSTEM OF NECESSITY.

IF all God's thoughts, purposes and plans existed from eternity, then they were as eternal and as uncreated as himself. If they were eternal and uncreated, they existed of necessity. If they were necessary, God did not originate them, and had no control over them. Admit this, and the system of necessity is immovably established, and inexorably controls not only all things, and all intelligent creatures, but also the Infinite One himself. All God's plans, purposes and feelings roll forth from necessity. In him there can be no exercise of free-will, and bald fatalism binds him this hour in all his life and creative acts, and in all his benefactions and governmental activities. But if God is a free being he can originate. If he originates, the thing he originates, previous to its origination, had no possible incipiency even in his conception. The activities of the divine Mind and the freedom of the divine Will necessarily imply that in the future, as in the past, God will ever go forth to creations of things absolutely new to himself for the perfection of his ideal universe, and for the elevation and the bliss of his intelligent millions. If God cannot now originate a new thought, he never could and never did. If he never did originate a new thought, all his thoughts were eternal and necessary. From this conclusion we all gladly take refuge in the thought that God can and does constantly originate thoughts and purposes and plans relative to a contingent objective universe, new even to himself. If absolutely new to himself, they cannot possibly be foreknown. Thus it is that only by divine nescience of future contingencies can we escape the dreadful and ever-darkening de-energizing system of necessity.

CHAPTER IV.

DIVINE NESCIENCE OF FUTURE CONTINGENCIES IS NECESSARY TO THE DIVINE PERFECTIONS.

MANY reasons can be adduced to prove that absolute prescience is not necessary to divine perfection. For our present purpose we will state but two. Had God never created any thing, he still would be absolutely perfect. In the second place, if the prescience of contingencies be necessary to the perfection of omniscience, then the existence of objective contingencies is necessary to that perfection. But this would make the perfection of omniscience to depend upon the existence of the objective, and not upon his subjective nature, which is manifestly absurd.

But you may reply that it is the power to foreknow future contingencies, and not the actual foresight, that is necessary to the perfections of omniscience. But as well may you say that the power to do all things is essential to the perfection of omnipotence. Yet there are things which it is impossible for Omnipotence to do; such as opening and shutting a door at the same instant of time, or creating a good character in the soul of one uniformly volitionating evil. But your affirmation that the power to foreknow is essential to the perfection of omniscience, is a mere assumption, for omniscience was absolutely perfect in the absence of all thought of future contingencies. But, on the other hand, if such manifest teachings of the Scriptures as the doctrine of endless punishment, sincere offers of life to all men, and the universal atonement for the race, be all true, then absolute prescience would be an imperfection in Deity, so grave as not only to overthrow God's moral government and to ruin his universe, but also to ruin, in all ways, the great I AM himself. Why should God entreat those to accept of his salvation who were foreknown to reject it?

But, on the other hand, divine nescience of future contingencies is positively necessary to the perfection of Deity. To his perfection as an intellect, as a thinker, as a heart, as a moral character, as a being of candor, as a Creator taking pleasure in his creatures and as a universal Ruler.

1. *Nescience is necessary to the perfection of the divine intellect.*

It is the instinct of all intelligent beings, however wicked they may be, to ascribe all perfections to the Deity. But man, being limited, may regard that a perfection which is really an imperfection. Having been created in the intellectual image of his Creator, he must have been originally a truthful illustration of that image. What is necessary to the perfection of the finite copy may confidently be looked for in the infinite model. Man possesses the susceptibilities of novelty, surprise, wonder, astonishment, sublimity, beauty and variety. Could all such implanted principles be removed from his nature and still he remain in the intellectual image of God? If not, then these susceptibilities must be qualities of the divine Mind. But how can God ever experience surprise, wonder, astonishment or unexpectedness, if free beings have not capacities, in their fathomless freedom, thus to surprise and delight the Father of the universe? Why does infinite variety reign everywhere if God does not dread everlasting monotony? It is the nature of mind to be active. It dreads inactivity and unbroken repose. It must be industrious, it must delight in originating, in creating, in meeting unlooked-for emergencies, in honoring unlooked-for drafts upon infinite mercy, and in accomplishing vast and various results by single efforts and simple agencies. But prescience makes the infinite intellect an inglorious idler from everlasting to everlasting, all his works having been accomplished in conception from eternity. He can intuit whatever exists, or exists in existing causes, but prescience makes him to intuit nonentities. But this being self-contradictory would be an imperfection in the divine intellect.

If I am capable of personic action, and can hold in sovereign control divine influences competing for my suffrage and service, then I am capable of alternative choices. Hence if God now knows all my future choices, he also knows all the alternate choices which I might, but which I may not, make. But this would fill the divine Mind with countless millions of worthless unrealities, and the intellect that can hold in its perpetual consciousness realities and unrealities, principles and non-principles, histories and non-histories, facts and non-facts equally definite, can neither be perfect, sound, safe, healthful, nor worthy of infinite adoration.

2. *Nescience necessary to God's perfection as a thinker.*

"All thought," says Sir William Hamilton, "is comparison." I do not myself see how this can be questioned. Our understanding is our comparing faculty. The greatest of man's achievements intellectually is the full development of the understanding. But prescience sweeps at once the great faculty of the understanding, the elaborative faculty and all logical influences out of the infinite Mind, and without the comparing faculty he has, and can have, no power of consecutive thinking. It would be impossible for him to place thoughts in a logical order or to think of things in their sources, dependencies, relations, consequences and possibilities. "God cannot know one thing before another, and one thing after another," says John Wesley. If this be so, then thinking in the abstract, generalizing, classifying, conceiving of the undetermined, estimating probabilities and following forces in their results and dependencies, are all with him impossibilities. Entrance upon the grand realms of the abstract is forever denied him. "There can be," says Dr. Jamison, "no succession of thoughts in the divine Mind." But God himself says, "I know the thoughts that I think toward you," they are "thoughts of peace, and not of evil." Jer. xxix, 11. "Even two volitions in succession," says Dr. Jamison, "would destroy the simplicity of the divine essence." If this be so, God makes worlds and burns them up, creates souls and binds them in everlasting chains, invites them to his love and fixes an impassable gulf between them and himself, and millions of other self-contradictory things, all in one and the same volition. Such tantalizing absurdities may be, and I suppose are, the logical sequiturs of the assumption of absolute prescience.

But nescience of future contingencies secures to Deity an intellect free from all such contradictions, and presents for our admiration a mind of unspeakable perfections, activities and resources, conceiving, imagining, inferring, calculating, originating and thinking with unutterable grandeur, and always to sure issues and with magnificent realizations.

3. *Nescience is necessary to the perfection of God's fatherly heart.*

"I have thought for years," said a worthy and thoughtful minister of Christ, "that if God now knows that I will be lost, it is already certain that I will be, and it is no relief to me to be told that foreknowledge does not necessitate my certain fate. It is the solemn fact that I will be lost that concerns me, rather than the agency by which my destiny is determined." This is perfectly natural, and it was the present uncertainty of his future destiny that aroused all his immortal energies to make his calling and election sure. So long as he believed his future to be now certain he was paralyzed into suspense and inactivity. If God is now certain that I will be lost, he knows that any further anxious, tender solicitude concerning me will be of no possible avail. It is impossible for him, in the nature of things, to feel relative to an immortal soul as he would necessarily feel were he in profound uncertainty over his future fate. The suspense, doubt, apprehension, alternation between hope and fear, and the fervent desires of infinite Benevolence relative to the endless destiny of his immortal child, which divine nescience requires, are indispensable to that tenderness of the infinite heart, and to that degree of parental solicitude and fatherly care which as a father he unquestionably owes to his deathless offspring, traveling the hazardous path of trial, to the judgment of the great day. God left Hezekiah on a certain occasion, it is said, (2 Chron. xxxii, 31,) to try him, that he might know all that was in his heart. God tried him in order to see what was in his heart. "Forty years," said Moses, "hath he led thee in the wilderness, to humble thee, and to prove thee, to know what was in thine heart, whether thou wouldest keep his commandments, or no." Here light for us breaks in on the feelings and workings of the infinite heart of the universal Father. How the anxious Father's heart is bewrayed into the expressions, "If therefore the light that is in thee be darkness, how great is that darkness," ... and "Let him that thinketh he standeth take heed lest he fall." "Oh that thou hadst hearkened to my commandments! then had thy peace been as a river, and thy righteousness as the waves of the sea."

4. *Nescience of contingencies is necessary to the perfection of God's moral character.*

The perfection of an ideal universe requires the creation of moral beings. By moral beings I mean beings who can be happy only from a consciousness of voluntary obedience. But if God foresees all contingencies he can create such free beings as he knows will choose obedience. In such a creation he would have an ideal universe, without the horrors and sorrows of endless perdition. Those he foresees will choose right, will choose it just as freely as the obedient do now choose it. In order to get free agents and all the moral sublimities of moral freedom and moral achievements into the universe, there was no necessity of creating souls he foreknew would be lost. Rewarding right-choosing free agents clearly implies law, penalty, government and the necessity of punishing wrong-choosing free agents. For choosing the right is always done under the conviction that choosing the wrong is not only inevitably but necessarily to be punished. By such a safeguarding of his moral universe all the ends of divine government, all the perfections of his creatures and all the effulgence of his throne, would have been amply secured without the creation of those he foreknows will choose disobedience, and be forever degraded and unhappy. God cannot be infinitely benevolent if he creates individual beings whom he foresees will be eternally miserable. He could not create such beings without a plan reaching from eternity to eternity, if prescience be true.

But no plan, purpose or consideration could ever justify such a procedure. Infinite benevolence would insist with a thousand imperative voices, rather than create individual souls foreknown to be eternally wretched, let no accountable creatures be created at all. Far better that multitudes should never know the boon of existence, or the rapture of basking forever in the beams of infinite wisdom and benevolence, than that one immortal soul should endure anguish and degradation forever. To me immortal existence has fathomless significations, and ever-increasing attractions, but notwithstanding this I would greatly prefer annihilation to seeing one of my children among the forever-lost—a fate to which I know they are now exposed. But what is my narrow, meager, limited benevolence, in comparison with the boundless benevolence of the Father of mercies? No plan that requires as a factor, your foreknown endless suffering, can ever be justified, at the bar of an infinitely perfect moral character. "Never would God have created men who were foreknown to be wicked," says Augustine, "had he not seen how they would finally subserve the ends of goodness." But, what ends of goodness could justify God in such a terrible creation? Create souls foreknown to be wicked in order to subserve the ends of goodness! What aid, vindication or illustration did goodness need? How could divine goodness be justified, much less vindicated, by creating souls foreknown to dwell in everlasting burnings?

If from all eternity God foresaw that you were

to be eternally miserable, and still, with all these terrible realities before him, he allowed you to come into existence, it is the baldest mockery for him now to ask you to obey and worship him, and to seek his favor and presence. But if an accountable being, unforeseen, chooses to be disobedient, then right, justice, universal order, the necessities of good government and the endless welfare and progressions of the moral universe, all demand inexorably his punishment. Between the sinner and his punishment God cannot interfere without violating immutable moral distinctions. Neither mercy nor benevolence dare ever to interfere. For endless separation of the incorrigible from the presence of God, in conscious existence, must be preferred, terrible as it must be, to the desolating march of universal anarchy throughout the moral universe. But would you not shudder through all the depths of your being to witness God in the act of creating an individual soul a feeble, limited creature who he knows will be degraded and suffer forever?

If the perfection o. divine goodness, and the desire to prevent suffering, and the desire to preserve his moral universe in moral beauty, do not necessitate divine nescience of future contingencies, then all human analogies, are simply worthless in any divine investigation. That a pure, happy, self-sufficient being, could desire, plan, bring about, permit or infallibly foreknow, all the iniquities, terrible scenes and sufferings of this world and the endless anguish of millions in the world to come, is a proposition that is too shocking for a sensibility developed, refined, enlightened and harmonized by the Gospel of God's grace.

No considerations, no ends, no final causes, could ever justify God, before an intelligent universe, in violating absolute rectitude, or in overriding freedom in free agents, or in outraging benevolence, either in planning wickedness, or in desiring its inception, or in creating individual souls who he foresaw would certainly be wicked and miserable and everlasting blotches upon his moral universe. Were I to allow my child to cross a bridge, after I had been variously assured she could not attempt it without meeting a most excruciating death, I should be justly execrated. Logic vouchsafes to me no safer inference than that nescience of contingencies is necessary to safeguard the moral character of Jehovah.

5. Nescience of future contingencies is necessary to safeguard the divine candor.

God said, "I set before you life and death, blessing and cursing; therefore choose ye life." If after this solemn address he had added, "But I know you will choose death, and all my arrangements are made up on your choice of death; I have made your choice of death a working factor in my future plans; upon that choice I have made thousands of predications, reaching in their influence round the globe and through all time;" could he in any way, I inquire, have so effectually eliminated all efficiency from their will-power and binding force from his commands? Could he in any other way have so thoroughly discouraged his struggling children, or enfeebled their purposes in their honest efforts to elect between eternal life and eternal death?

And if he certainly foreknew their choices candor sternly required of him to make it known to them. In uttering this heart-felt entreaty he clearly assumes that he does not foreknow their ultimate choices. "God teaches us," says Rudolf Stier, "Matt. xxi, 37, that he makes trial of goodness in men just as he would did he not know beforehand in what cases it will prove in vain." And in this entreaty God certainly assumes that there is valid ground for the alternation between the alternates of obedience and disobedience. And if *he* assumes it, how dare any creature call it in question? "A capacity for alternate action," says L. P. Hickok, "or a cause which has an alternative, is itself no ground for determining which of the two shall come to pass." Now, if there was not in this command any ground for alternation between the choices, then the command was cruel and double-dealing in the extreme.

If a future event is now certain it is unreasonable in Deity to implore me to change from the choice of sin to the choice of holiness. "It is for us," says Dr. Chalmers, "to do strenuously that which God has commanded, and never allow ourselves to think of what *he* knows relative to our future, for these are mysteries too deep for us." But Christians in multitudes, in all evangelical Churches, live in the most intimate and tender fellowship, secret understanding and delightful oneness with the Father of their spirits. But how incongruous with this state of grace and nearness to God that the devout soul should never enter into questionings relative to God's knowledge of its endless well-being or misery? God simply trifles with me if he commands me to choose and to act in reference to that which to me is an uncertainty, but which to him is a positive certainty. To affirm that God requires me to act as though an infallible certainty were an actual uncertainty is simply blasphemous toward God and paralyzing toward all my moral energies. Should God command me to act as though the morrow's sun were an uncertainty he could not play a part with more heartless insincerity. God calls me to act promptly, under his moral government, with an earnestness that is unspeakable; and yet, if prescience be true, I can never act as a probationer for eternity but under the inspiration of an unquestioned delusion that my future choices are now real uncertainties, and that it is now possible for me to do an impossible thing, namely, to change my infallibly foreknown destiny. No learning, no greatness, no ingenuity, can ever defend from ignominy the divine candor if absolute foreknowledge be true.

6. Nescience is necessary to God as a Creator taking happiness in his creatures.

God takes pleasure in every thing that he makes. If moral government has any significance, it means smiles for the obedient and frowns for the disobedient. It means the divine presence for the moral hero, and the divine absence for the incorrigible. If the Ruler sees all the future as he sees the present, then he is the subject of the most conflicting emotions of approval and disapproval toward every individual of the race. He is subject to this conflict of emotions at every moment of time, corresponding to every variety of conduct and changes in the moral character of his creatures. But how can God entertain such conflicts of emotions, such contrarieties of contemporaneous feelings, at every moment, without disturbing the harmonies and the equanimities of his eternally blessed and blissful nature?

Once God frowned upon me, and I felt his frown burning into my soul. It was a terrible reality with me because it was a terrible reality with God. Now God approves of me, and no angel words can express the delight I find in his presence and smile. His feelings toward me now, and his feelings toward me when I was an impenitent sinner, if there be no succession with him, would be crowded into the same moment and into the same experience. And that which is true of me is true of the countless millions of my race.

If prescience be true, God can take no enjoyment in creatures morally so vacillating and imperfect. But divine nescience shelters us from all such absurdities, and shields Deity from such imperfections in his heart-experience and continuous life.

God's present feelings toward me are those of a Father. I am trying to obey him. There is now no shadow between him and my soul. Jesus Christ reigns in my heart; his blood is cleansing me, and the Holy Ghost is carrying forward the sublime work of my recreation in the divine image unto good works. But if God now knows that eventually I will apostatize, all such fatherly feelings would be utterly impossible. Adam fell out of Paradise, and Satan fell out of heaven from a place hard by the throne; and God says to me, "Let him that thinketh he standeth take heed lest he fall."

7. *Nescience is necessary to God's perfection as a Ruler.*

For the infinite Cause of all things to rule the universe by the law of cause and effect presents to him no difficulties. To rule accountable beings when all their acts are foreknown presents few if any more difficulties than to rule in the realm of material forces. Foreknowing every determination of every free being, with all their attendant circumstances and influences near and remote, he can arrange for them as easily as he can control a planet bursting into fragments.

But the great perfection and boundless resources and unutterable glories of a Ruler are brought out and set forth in ruling a universe of independent, accountable beings, of whose countless choices he never can be forecertain. How his power, wisdom, goodness, ubiquity, watchfulness, care for his universe, tenderness for the loyal, jealousy for the law, desire for good government, interest in morality and religion, and solicitude for the well-being of his sensitive creatures, all shine forth in transcendent brightness as he meets the millions of emergencies thrust upon him every moment by the unforeseen choices of responsible beings!

How ennobling a view does this statement present to us of the divine sovereignty! How meager, perplexing and offending the divine sovereignty which foreknowledge or foreordination has to offer for our contemplation. Foreordination deliberately outlaws all contingencies from the divine government. Foreknowledge assures us that there are such things as contingencies, but that God does not possess resources sufficiently ample to safely manage them without having absolutely certain prevision of them. Compared to eternity, time is but a moment and earth but a pebble in God's boundless domains; and yet they think him incapable of meeting the emergencies of a period so brief and on a theater so limited.

The grandeur of the divine sovereignty which is here advocated, and requiring divine nescience of future contingencies, immeasurably transcends in glory that presented by either the advocates of prescience or of predestination. What unspeakable glories burst forth from the divine sovereignty as we behold the infinite Ruler adjudicating on myriads of arenas countless individual cases with all the precision, forms, and solemnities of forensic procedures, and instantly administering rewards and punishments therefor! In comparison how pitiful the divine sovereignty of the advocate of predestination, election, preterition or of absolute prescience. Calvinian divine sovereignty is reckless of every thing else in theological thought.

The divine sovereignty here presented is a sovereignty over sovereigns, not a sovereignty over mere machines or passive instruments, under the reign of mechanical philosophy. With many unmistakable voices God is now saying to me, " I do not absolutely know what you, as a free being, will sovereignly choose in my kingdom of free grace, but I am a most deeply interested spectator of your conduct on the great moral battle-fields for eternity. I was absolutely forced to run a momentous risk when I made you a free being, and you must run a solemn risk in making your endless destiny. But there is no necessity of any miscarriage as to your immortal interests. I will stand by you with my immortal strength in every moment of the fight. If you do right I will reward you in ways innumerable; but persistent wrong-doing and incorrigible disobedience must necessarily separate you eternally from my glorious presence. I have a specific plan for you, but that plan is conditioned wholly upon your obedience to the many and mighty voices of duty. The excellencies and advantages of that plan you cannot now conceive, and I cannot now reveal. But if you sovereignly choose to infract that plan by persistent disobedience, I am here to maintain justice, to sustain order, to give full significancy to law and all its penalties, and to carry forward, from height to height, the perfections of my moral government. If the contradictions, perplexities, bewilderments and enervations inseparable from prescience and predestination could be swept out of existence, and every man could hear such direct appeals as the above from his Creator, the world would be half converted while I am speaking.

No ruler ought to be angry with a subject before he has violated his law. But prescience makes God sit in judgment on me, sentence me, adjust my punishment, arrange for my endless abode in perdition with Satan, long before I committed the least offense against his law. How absurd a ruler who can find it in his heart to be angry with one before that one has felt a rebellious emotion! If I am the creator of my own moral character it is cruel in God to regard me as hateful before my character is such. The Calvinian expresses a hurricane of resentment when told that he teaches the damnation of infants, but the prescient Arminian teaches the damnation of the infant millions of ages before it was an infant. I would as lief be damned out of my cradle as to be damned myriads of years before my mother folded me so tenderly therein.

God's perfection as a ruler requires that his treatment of his subjects should vary with the ever-varying character of their volitions and moral attitudes. This is absolutely indispensable. Any other view of his governmental relations makes him so inconsistent, unnatural and despotic that he is an object to be dreaded rather than loved and adored. How can it be that all do not see that the perfection and splendors of the divine Ruler and Sovereign actually demand divine nescience of future contingencies? Nescience presents to us the sovereignty of God with most impressive magnificence as he goes forth over the boundless universe overcoming all difficulties, and arresting, as far as possible, all evils which are inevitable in the government of beings whose choices originate in the depths of their own free-wills. Besides, if God meet with no difficulties in the management of his empires of accountable beings, how can he perfectly sympathize with us in our great and hazardous difficulties in working out our eternal destiny, escaping a world of unending darkness, and finally, through boundless mercy, reaching a world of ineffable light?

CHAPTER V.

NESCIENCE OF CONTINGENCIES IS NECESSARY TO SAFEGUARD THE WISDOM AND CANDOR OF THE HOLY GHOST.

THE Holy Ghost sees now that I am certainly to be lost, if that fate awaits me and prescience be true. From all eternity he has distinctly seen my awful doom. He not only saw me entering the arena of life, but he saw himself entering it with me. He saw himself breathing holy influences upon me when the atmosphere first bathed me, when the light first saluted me, and when my mother pressed me for the first time to her throbbing breast. He saw himself watching tenderly my orphan footsteps, and then with enhanced interest and solicitude as I crossed the line of accountability, and encountered the fearful hazards of a homeless youth.

From all eternity he has seen himself laboring with me, illuminating me, wooing me, beseeching me not to grieve him, not to wrong my own soul, but to be holy and obedient. He has seen himself making these persistent efforts, to describe which even angelic eloquence would be incompetent, and yet from all eternity he has foreknown that he would in the end signally fail in all his endeavors to snatch my soul from endless perdition.

He has always known that I would be finally an incorrigible outcast; and yet he has been laboring for my redemption with all the vehemence of infinite love. But what sensible man would remain at the foot of Mont Blanc for half a century, making unceasing efforts to remove it from its base by the breath of his mouth? Equally unreasonable and indefensible is it for the Holy Ghost to make incessant efforts, through decades of years, to rescue from eternal ruin one whose name has ever been enrolled on the immutable records of absolute prescience on the dark scroll of fate, and spoken of and calculated upon in all the counsels of eternity, as a vessel of wrath and an heir of death. All the awakenings, illuminatings, renewings, strivings and inspirings which the Holy Ghost has wrought in my sinful soul were wrought there on the clearly assumed fact of my actual avoidability of moral evil. He has made me think and feel that he himself really thinks and feels, that there is for me now an unquestioned avoidability of eternal death. What he has done for me he has done for all men, for "He is the light that enlighteneth every man that cometh into the world." But is it possible that the Holy Ghost should come to me as though he came in good faith, dealing with me in all candor, entreating me not to quench his light, not to sin, but to embrace his offer of salvation, when at that very moment he knows that he has already predicated ten thousand specific results and enterprises upon my foreknown choice of resisting him, unto eternal death, and when, too, he knows my choice of death is indispensable to safeguard his own infallible foreknowledge?

If such views and beliefs do not stultify and dishonor the third person of the adorable Trinity, and render insincere and mockish all his efforts to rescue from ruin perishing souls, then the human mind may instanter abandon thinking as a means of reaching reliable conclusions on any religious subject. But the above inferences are no more startlingly *blasphemous*, than they are logically inevitable from the undue assumption of absolute prescience. Better surrender prescience at any hazard, than to fasten insincerity upon the Holy Ghost, whom the Father hath sent in the name of his Son.

CHAPTER VI.

DIVINE NESCIENCE OF FUTURE CONTINGENCIES IS A NECESSITY TO ESCAPE THE CRUSHING SYSTEM OF PANTHEISM.

OF all the foes with which Christianity has now to contend, pantheism is the direst. It is a system so subtle, plausible, complete, capable of varying its aspects and applications, and so flattering to the pride of the human intellect, that it exerts over multitudes of thinkers a strange power of fascination. But no error, philosophical, theological or ethical, is so variously demoralizing. All its fundamental propositions are false. All its ground assumptions are fallacious, and all its definitions are arbitrary, antagonistic to reason, and without the authority vouchsafed by our intuitions. It identifies existence with thought, the laws of thought with the laws of being, and binds all things and themes in the brazen fetters of fatalism. It annihilates moral distinctions, affirms that might is the only measure and umpire of right, repudiates moral government, and patronizingly smiles at the puerile thought of a human accountability. It eliminates every thing that is morally positive in the nature of wickedness, destroys in the soul the conviction of sin which was wrought there by the Holy Ghost, and resolutely calls iniquity an inconceivability. It robs man of his personality, strips him of self-hood, batters down the distinction between him and the brute, and leaves him no place for his faith, his trust, his hope, his support. It paralyzes all springs in his soul, checks all aspirations and inspirations in his spirit, removes all restraints from before his appetites and passions, renders speechless his conscience, the queen of his faculties, and derives not a single motive from the future world for his self-control. Knowing that the system would commit suicide were it to admit the possibility of creation, it vehemently denies all possibility thereof. It identifies unintelligent, unsusceptible nature with her glorious Creator. It makes the whole universe of mind and matter a simple substance or being. It blends finite minds into the infinite mind or substance. To Deity it denies all personality, declaring him to be destitute of freedom. It is more degrading and ruinous than even atheism itself. It is, indeed, the worst form of atheism. It being so revolting to the human soul outright to deny the existence of God, Pantheism volunteers to utter the offending affirmation surreptitiously, Judas-like betraying with a kiss of deception the God of the whole earth. " Pantheism," says one, " is the ghost of atheism, sitting defiantly upon its tombstone."

The influence of this bucklered competitor of our holy religion is now greatly on the increase, through the agency, it is vehemently claimed, of German philosophy. The Jew Spinoza gave to pantheism its substance, Emanuel Kant gave to it its form. The philosophy of Kant determined, to a very large extent, the character of all the subsequent speculations in Germany. Schelling and Hegel were the greatest and the most faithful of all the disciples of Spinoza. They were far-reaching in their pantheistic influence over Germany and general literature. And at this writing authors of sedate character, familiar with the practical influences of pantheistic philosophy, theology, exegesis, ethics and politics, express grave apprehensions of our ultimate return to paganism and polytheistic worships, unless some salutary check be presented to this monstrous error, the most formidable of all the rivals of Christianity.

But, if absolute prescience be true, it is impossible for God to put forth or to originate a simple volition new to himself. All the volitions he ever put forth, all that he ever will put forth, were known to him from all eternity. If they were all known to him from eternity they were as eternal as himself. If they were as eternal as himself he could not have originated them; he could not have originated them any more than he could originate himself. But if he did not originate his volitions he cannot have a free-will. If he has not a free-will he cannot be a person. If he is not a person he must be impersonal, if he really exists at all. If he is impersonal he must be without consciousness. If he is without consciousness and has a real existence, he must be without moral character or moral force or sympathy. He must be controlled in all his activities and movements, from eternity to eternity, wholly by blind but inexorable necessity. If this be so, then the pantheistic theory of Deity is established beyond controversy, and the Christian religion is absolutely vanquished and driven from the field. If pantheism is true, the whole universe of contingencies is at once swept out of existence. All moral distinctions, moral government, human responsibility are meaningless propositions. Moral night, without a single star of hope to illumine the awful future, broods far and wide over an abandoned world and a bankrupt humanity. Grant to the pantheist your undue assumption of absolute prescience, and he asks and needs no more. Never after that can you break the merciless chain with which he first binds you, and then proceeds to spoil this glorious house of the almighty Father of the universe.

But, on the other hand, affirm divine nescience of future contingencies, and one of you can chase a hundred pantheists, and two put ten thousand to flight. How grandly nescience rescues us from all the horrors of degrading desolating pantheism, who can express, and the necessity of nescience, who can adequately estimate? Assume prescience, and pantheism is inevitable. Assume nescience, and the divine personality can never be assailed.

CHAPTER VII.

DIVINE NESCIENCE OF FUTURE CONTINGENCIES IS NECESSARY TO GIVE VALIDITY TO OUR HOPES AND FEARS.

WHEN God proclaims "He that endureth unto the end, the same shall be saved," he inspires in all men a hope of heaven. When he says, " Be not afraid of them that can kill the body, and after that have no more that they can do, but fear him, who after that he hath killed, hath power to cast into hell ; " and when he says, " Fear him who is able to destroy both soul and body in hell," he intends to awaken in all the emotion of fear. If the human soul was created with the susceptibilities of hope and fear, then there must be reliable grounds for their exercise. If there be no such grounds, then the Creator endowed us with these susceptibilities simply to delude us, or to induce us to act under palpable delusions. All know the potent nature of these implanted passions in the formation of character, in the achievements of destiny, and in the endurance of hardships. But if the future is now an infallible certainty, there cannot be any reliable arena for their truthful exercise. Neither hope nor fear can logically or reasonably exert any influence upon him who really believes that the future is now fixed and certain. If the future of each soul is now with God an infallible certainty, there is no possible ground for the Calvinian elect to fear, and none for the Calvinian non-elect to hope. But how, in good faith or in fatherly candor or in common honesty, can God inspire me with a hope of immortal life, which most emphatically I know he has done, when he knows at the very moment he does so my eternal death is an infallible certainty? How can he distress and appall me and often overwhelm me, as I know he does, with the fear of my becoming a castaway, when he knows that I am absolutely certain of a crown of life? This appalling apprehension of final apostasy was perhaps the terrible thorn in his flesh from which St. Paul thus besought divine deliverance. We thus see that prescience undermines, and cannot but undermine, all the valid grounds for the exercise of hope and fear, those powerful susceptibilities of the human soul. How erroneous must a doctrine be that renders mendacious and illusory the godlike attributes of the mind! And with what an odious character of insincerity, pretense and double-dealing does such a doctrine invest the Father of mercies, who, while tenderly inspiring me with the hope of eternal life, knows from all eternity that I am to be a vessel of wrath, fitted for everlasting destruction. For God thus to inspire me is simply an instance of cruel duplicity, unparalleled in the realms of deception, secret will, finesse and heartlessness. I have a family of children for whom I have labored, sacrificed, watched incessantly, prayed, and often bedewed my pillow and my path with tears, that they might at last escape eternal death. I have waited and hoped and sighed for their salvation ever since their existence began. The care has been constant and the burden onerous. Now, if God has known that they were to be eternally lost ought he not, in justice as well as in mercy to me, who would prefer death to offending him, to have unveiled to me the awful destiny that awaits them? Could a just God allow one whose aim is to please him, to carry for so many years a burden so overwhelming and at the same time so utterly needless? Could he allow me to be so deluded with cherished hopes of an unbroken family circle in the eternal light of his favor, all of which are without the slighest foundations? How universal prescience does degrade the glorious God, in annihilating all the foundations of eternal hopes and of fears! If it does not, then may we well abandon all manly thinking.

There is ground for fear that finally I may be numbered with outcasts forever. There is ground for hope, through unsearchable mercy, that I may yet reach and sing with the ransomed. God now fears I may be lost, but hopes I may be redeemed. These same hopes and fears fill my soul, and are the springs of my fervent spiritual activities. Theologians, do not, I entreat you, paralyze all my immortal, redeemed energies, by telling me that God now infallibly foreknows that I am to be eternally banished from his glorious presence.

CHAPTER VIII.

DIVINE NESCIENCE OF CONTINGENCIES IS NECESSARY TO THE IMPRESSION THAT OUGHT TO BE MADE ON THE MIND OF A PROBATIONER FOR ETERNITY.

IF my endless future be now pending, the most impressive view of my responsibility that possibly can be taken ought to be presented for my calm consideration. That view of my case which can most thoroughly arouse and inspire me to put forth volitional energy to escape a sad and to win a bright destiny, is my *inalienable* birthright as a probationer for eternity, accountable at the bar of the universe.

Suppose your dying at nightfall is an event dependent upon your own will, and that you believe that it is now certain in the divine mind whether you will or will not die at nightfall. Can this belief that the event is already a certainty in the mind of God fail to lessen the definiteness and energy of your volitions? Will it not depress the energies of your freedom? If it does not, then no conceivable belief can exert any detrimental and enervating influence upon your determinations. It would, therefore, be a matter of no moment at all what opinions men are taught, advocate or embrace. And, upon this supposition, St. Paul's great tenacity for sound doctrines, so frequently expressed, was wholly uncalled-for, if not unjustifiable.

But, on the other hand, suppose it is now uncertain in the divine mind whether you will or will not die at nightfall, that it is an event lying wholly within the purview of your own freedom, will not the belief that with God the event is now uncertain nerve your will-power to determine against dying at nightfall, and to translate your resolution into history? To this question reason can return but a single response. Belief in the present certainty of a future event always enervates, or more or less weakens the will which is to be the sole author of that event. The *uncertainty* of a future event most powerfully arouses and animates the autocrat of the soul to meet his greatest requirement and to realize his greatest fruition. This is the testimony of uniform consciousness.

Divine nescience of contingencies is necessary to give validity to our religious consciousness. It is necessary to a full conception of the true greatness of the human soul, and to a complete idea of its personal responsibility for unending results. It is necessary to the highest inspiration of which we are susceptible, and to the completest unfolding of the fathomless resources and capacities of our moral freedom. Divine nescience of future contingencies takes human choices out of foreordination, out of fatality, out of constraint, out of the enervating influences of foreknowledge, and out of all metaphysical mysteries, and places them just where they really and rightfully belong, in the free originative capacity of a responsible man. And to this *view*, this presentation of the case, the human soul, as an accountable agent, has an inalienable birthright, founded in the profundities of eternal justice. The theologies of the world have, however, shriveled into insignificance and paralyzed into imbecility the stupendous capacities of human liberty. They have not only slandered the Almighty, but they palsied humanity. Prescience hides from the probationer the profoundest and most moving views of his own capacities, and to these views he has blood-bought claims, bought on the cross by his adorable Redeemer.

CHAPTER IX.

DIVINE NESCIENCE OF FUTURE CONTINGENCIES IS NECESSARY TO AN INTERPRETATION OF THE HOLY SCRIPTURES.

NO profound believer in the awful verities of the holy Scriptures will question the necessity of the correct, consistent and speedy interpretation of its essential and heaven-inspiring teachings. There are innumerable passages in these sacred writings which express, and more which imply, the positive constraint of the human will, and in which the human will is placed under the law of cause and effect. The passages which express and imply the freedom of the human will, and that it acts freely under the law of liberty, and not under the law of constraint, are equally innumerous. These facts necessitate the existence of two kingdoms, in one of which God works all things after the counsel of his own sovereign will, and in the other he works and overrules and administers in accordance with the free volitions of accountable beings. In the kingdom of providence, by which we mean God's watchful, provident care over sensitive beings, he works results and accomplishes his purposes by constraint of the human will. In the management of the affairs of this world this kingdom is indispensable every hour. Men are continually used by God as instruments in the accomplishment of his providential purposes. In the kingdom of free grace God works and coworks with free agents. He rewards, punishes, subjugates or glorifies them in accordance with their moral character. But in the kingdom of providence God treats man as an instrument. In the kingdom of free grace he deals with him as a sovereign person. The only theory that can safeguard Scripture is, that in the utterance of prophecy and in its fulfillment God treats man not as a person, but simply as an instrument. There are two classes of Scripture prophecies, the conditional and the unconditional. The unconditional are those that refer to the divine purposes, and which God brings about either by his own direct efforts or by employing intelligent beings as instruments in his hands. No unconditional prophecy ever fails of fulfillment. The conditional prophecies are made upon the condition of the voluntary compliance of free agents with certain specified terms and conditions. "Many prophecies," says Dr. Dorner, "fail of their fulfillment." Of course any failure in the fulfillment of prophecy is confined to the conditional class of prophecies.

Every theologian must keep distinctly before his mind the grand distinction of man as an instrument and man as a responsible person. If he does not, he will inevitably become confused in his thoughts, and hesitating in his utterances. A person, as we have said, is a being who can elect between competing motives, and then absolutely originate resolves. So long as the great doctrines of election and reprobation are maintained, the Bible must remain a book flooded with confessed contradictions, and what are called, by Dr. Robert Breckenridge, "Bible paradoxes," which never can be explained by mortals. No learning, mental resources, logical acumen, or devoutness of spirit, have yet been able to free divine revelation from these ignominious, irritating and overwhelming inconsistencies. And thus must it ever be so long as foreordination is maintained.

These contradictions worry, perplex, enfeeble, confound, and often drive into stark infidelity, those who commenced the search of the word of God as sincere and devout inquirers. How discouraging it must be, for example, for a logical, discriminating mind, candidly inquiring after the truth, to hear, in a single sermon from Dr. J. W. Alexander, one of the finest of scholars, and the loveliest of men, that "the Scriptures expressly ascribe sinful acts to divine Providence, that God arranges the wicked act, adopts it into his providential plan, and yet puts forth no causative influence to its commission; that God is not the author of sin, yet nevertheless the sin occurs providentially; that God hates moral evil, and has no participation in it; and yet those who disbelieve and rebel are swayed by his providence; that all thoughts, feelings, frames and free acts, are controlled by infinite Wisdom; and that man acts freely, while God works out his irresistible decrees. We do not deny that there are difficulties here, but they arise from the depth of the divine nature and the short sounding line of human reason."

" The short sounding line of human reason " is certainly long enough to determine that it is impossible to establish " irresistible decrees," without tearing down the distinction between virtue and vice. The only way for the Calvinian to escape this axiom in theology, is to jump into a bank of mystery, and affirm, " We are very limited beings, indeed we are." But all the Scriptures which Dr. Alexander adduces in support of such contradictory declarations are susceptible of interpretations that are simple, cogent, and wholly unembarrassed by any self-contradictions. " The wicked act of selling Joseph into Egypt," he says, " was all arranged and formed a part of God's plan." Now which is easier to believe, that God did arrange that wicked act of selling, or that he had his own providential plan, irrespective of the wicked acts of Joseph's brethren, of sending him into Egypt in the interests of pure benevolence, and which he would have carried out had his brethren acted righteously? It is very easy to discriminate between a benevolent mission to Egypt and the mode or instrument of his conveyance there. God arranged for Joseph to go down to Egypt, but he did not plan that he should go there by fraternal wickedness.

" There never was a more vile act than the death of Christ," says Dr. Alexander, " and yet it was not only provided for, but it was indispensably necessary to the salvation of men. The act was wicked, but it was declared to be by the determinate counsel and fore-knowledge of God; therefore wicked acts are included in the plans of Providence."

True, to save a lost world, the death of Christ was by the determinate counsel and foreknowledge of God. But the *mode* of his death, by wicked men on a Roman cross, was nowhere attested, or even hinted at in the Old Testament Scriptures. Now which is easier to believe, that God planned the murder of Christ, or to distinguish between the necessity of the fact of his dying to save the world and the contingent mode and instrument of his dying? God had his own plan for the offering up of his Son, which wicked men murderously invaded, and wholly in opposition to his wishes. In this unutterable wickedness they could have desisted at any moment in their march up to Calvary. And they could have thus desisted without defeating the glorious work of redeeming the world. For Paul says they never would have crucified the Lord of life had they known "the hidden wisdom." Surely the multitudes now studying the word of God ought not to be confused and embarrassed and disheartened by a continuation of such unreasonable interpretations thereof, when interpretations so much more natural, obvious and unobjectionable, are ready for our consideration and acceptance. Such interpretations signal us from every side and quarter of thorough exegesis. Surely it is unwise any longer to palsy our faith in necessary inexplicables, by demanding the acceptance of beliefs that manifestly are so repugnant to human reason and benevolent impulses. "Such beliefs," said Benjamin Franklin, "are so repulsive that none do believe them, unless they have been patiently drilled into them from early childhood by revered parents." The Calvinian himself embraces them only because he feels compelled to do so in order to escape what he regards as a more unreasonable, inadmissible and ruinous position.

Some reader might possibly reply, " The doctrine of the Trinity is seemingly as self-contradictory as the doctrine of fore-ordination." But the inexplicity of the Trinity arises solely from the inability to comprehend the divine essence. We rejoice in this our inability; for were we able to comprehend the divine essence, it would not be worthy of our adoration.

But the difficulty we experience in believing the doctrine of predestination arises from our perception of the utter incompatibility between two easily comprehended propositions. God fore-ordains whatever comes to pass, and Man is a free agent, are two comprehensible propositions. And the more clearly they are separately comprehended, the more striking does their incompatibility appear. Between self-contradictions and mysteries there are no parallels, and none should parallelogistically be assumed in the defense of any thought system. It cannot be done without an ultimate breakdown to the system, unless men cease investigating, and inquiring the why and the wherefore.

The assumption of absolute foreknowledge may possibly lessen the number and heinousness of these inexplicable Scripture contradictions. But such an assumption necessitates principles of interpretation that will prevent our comprehension of the truth, the completeness, the naturalness, the consistency and the force of the divine word. This assumption must prevent any consistent or comforting conceptions of the character of God. It will prevent also the construction of a system of theology, without incorporating into it vexations, absurdities and ever-bothering perplexities. Such an assumption flatly ignores those principles of hermeneutics which are indispensable to any sound and consistent exegesis of the holy Scriptures.

Foreknowledge may relieve itself theoretically of some of the difficulties of fore-ordination, but it can never by any possible means escape the many and great difficulties of subsequent ordination. Free volitions become active working factors throughout the eternity, subsequent to their birth and existence. Foreseeing such things as independent volitions, God must determine how he will treat them, how he will reward, punish, control, or utilize them in maintaining his administration, in carrying forward his universal moral government, and in evolving and compassing his own eternal plans and purposes. This necessitates one vast system of subsequent ordination, assignment or prearrangement following necessarily from the assumption of divine foreknowledge. All future free choices being now infallibly foreknown, they are, and necessarily must be, immutable fixities. "They are all permanently adopted," says Dr. Whedon, "into the divine plan." And all the divine determinations and assignments and referrings, relative to those free choices being now infallible, the whole future is one vast fixity, as immutable in itself, as discouraging to freedom, as disheartening to hope, as enervating to the formation of individual moral character, and the putting forth of holy resolves, as any system of unalterable decree could ever possibly be. How inexcusable then is the vaulting assumption of the Arminian triumph, over the Calvinian dogma of eternal reprobation.

We see that foreknowledge unavoidably necessitates a divine comprehensive plan, reaching from eternity to eternity, linking every free choice with innumerable other events and things. It necessitates a plan, which involves the endless ruin of uncounted millions of sensitive immortal beings, every one of whom has his place and his mission and his influence, all over the moral universe and all through eternity. But every invitation, every entreaty, every promise and every threatening, addressed to me in the holy Scriptures implies my avoidability of sin. But if in the mind of God there is no contingency as to the coming to pass of my future free choice, the Bible is the most confusing, misleading, uncandid volume in all the literatures of the world. It is an inexplicable book upon the assumption of either fore-ordination or subsequent ordination, of predestination or of absolute prescience.

So long as one revered body of divines maintains that the human will always acts under the law of constraint, and the other great body of divines, equally revered and influential, maintains that the human will always acts under the law of liberty, there cannot possibly be harmony among theologians and commentators. The Bible, therefore, must remain inexplicable and unsatisfactory as to fundamental and essential teachings, and Christians must, as in the past, continue to cower and beg in craven confusion before the searching analysis and defiant arraignments of a candid and intelligent and inquiring unbelief.

For, evidently, the great system of Calvinian theology rests on the *self-contradiction*, man is free, but really and in fact without the power of contrary choice, all his choices being really constrained, *ab extra* or *ab intra*, by motives or subtle influences. And the great system of Arminianism rests on unthinkables equally manifest and patience-testing. Man, it says, is free, but all his future choices are now infallibly certain in themselves, and immutably assigned to the accomplishment of immutable results in an immutable universe throughout an immutable eternity.

Believers in divine revelation must ever submit to the taunts of infidels to agree in interpretation among themselves as to the fundamental teachings of divine revelation, and to furnish them with an exegesis that will not necessitate interminable perplexities and mental resentments. Every Calvinian knows that he meets with multitudes of passages whose Arminian look greatly perplexes him. He is often made to hesitate and wonder if his theory be really true, though so venerable with age and authority. President Nott said, "I believe both Calvinism and Arminianism, for manifestly both are taught in the word." In this he has been followed by multitudes of distinguished Calvinists, such, for example, as the clear-headed and charming Dr. Charles Simeon, who says, "There is not a single Calvinian or a single Arminian who approves equally of the whole of the Scriptures. Had either of them been with St. Paul he would have urged him to alter some of his expressions." He who believes in the third order of the ministry, and that the Methodist Discipline was written to teach the doctrine of prelacy, can never understand that wonderful system of ecclesiastical polity. He who believes in the divine right of kings and that the Constitution of the United States was established to sustain the divine royalty of the ruling classes, can never understand that remarkable instrument, the growth of so many ages. And, in like manner, no one who believes in the doctrine of election and reprobation can thoroughly understand the Scriptures unless that doctrine be clearly taught therein. But that doctrine is at best, as all confess, an uneasiness-producing doctrine. It makes all hesitate as to its being true, and to wonder if it can be true. Indeed, it is a belief that is ever attended with a penetrating regret that it is true. Even Augustine, sixteen hundred years ago, in thinking on his system, exclaimed relative to it, "Believe me, I am pressed with great perplexities." And this distrust evidently is the present trend of the convictions of the universal religious consciousness of the world. "After the Synod of Dort," says Bishop Burgess, "Calvinism grew fainter and fainter in the Church of England, till it scarcely struggled."

But if Paul really teaches the universality of the atonement, and the divine sincerity in the offers of eternal life to all reprobates, how can the stanch believer in election ever be able to comprehend him? Paul was either an Arminian or a Calvinian, and he taught the doctrine of one or the other. I think he uses the term "Προοριζω" to mean outlining a general plan or purpose. But the Calvinian understands by it God's arbitrary decree as to the endless destinies of souls. By the term *righteousness* Paul means holiness or purity of the soul, but the Calvinian understands by it the active or passive obedience of Jesus Christ imputed to a sinner. He regards righteousness as the robes of Christ's righteousness wrapped about the elect. By the term *justification* Paul means the forensic acquittal of the repenting sinner, on the ground of the unquestioned sincerity of his penitence; but the Calvinist understands it to mean his acquittal on the ground of God's sovereign and eternal decree. With the Calvinist faith is a consent to the covenant of grace, through which consent the sinner receives the benefit of justification. God pardons all the sins of the elect and accepts of them as righteous, because the active and passive righteousness of Christ is imputed to them. Imputed righteousness implies the absence of righteousness in the being to whom it is imputed.

Salvation by faith never was comprehended or apprehended by Augustine. With him "faith was only holding as true the phenomena of the life of Jesus." And this lack of a full and proper conception of a present saving, cleansing faith, is, it seems to me, the great and sad defect of Calvinian teachings. I have read Calvin's Institutes in a vain search for some evidence against this statement.

In the rigidities of Christian duty, and fulfilling all outward righteousness, the Calvinistic mind has been surpassed by none in the history of the Church. But in the spiritual liberties, joys and beatitudes of religious experience it is not uncharitable to think it greatly deficient. Self-condemnation, fear, distrust, uncertainty, apprehension of not being quite right, dread of spiritual pride, and horror of religious enthusiasm, have generally characterized this type of Christianity. And it is all traceable to the grave fact that its faith in Jesus, as a present and an all-sufficient Saviour, is neither Lutheran nor Pauline. "The Lutheran doctrine of faith was wholly unknown in the age of Augustine," says Dr. Wiggers.

So long as a man believes in the irresistibility of divine grace, eternal election and reprobation, the imputation to himself of Adam's personal guilt, and the imputation of the active and passive righteousness of Jesus Christ as the ground of his justification, his faith is too little concerned with the subjective relations which the unsaved soul sustains to the Saviour. The consciousness of such a one seldom, if ever, embraces those well-defined spiritual experiences and discriminations which always precede the gift of the power of saving faith, and those experiences that ever attend that faith that brings immediate pardon and sanctification through the all-cleansing blood, the faith that makes the soul conscious of God, conscious of God even as it is conscious of itself. The faith of such a one is too objective, too intellectual, in its embrace of formularies, and too foreign to spiritual necessities, to be truly evangelical or thoroughly saving or definitely experiential. And hence it is that the most gifted and cultured of the Calvinistic teachers are less distinct in their perceptions, and less definite and confident in their utterances upon the subject of the processes and the wonders of personal holiness than, perhaps, upon any other gospel theme. Therefore, the good and great Chalmers, while descanting upon the most precious doctrine of the direct witness of the Holy Spirit, exclaimed, "If there be such a direct witness of the Holy Spirit to one's justification, I know nothing of it myself experimentally." The confident affirmation and rejoicing of the Cavinistic mind that its faith is Pauline, certainly requires an unprejudiced re-examination. A clear and complete vision of the gospel of salvation can never be obtained, I am convinced, by Calvinistic principles or processes or modes of conception. "We are not commanded," says Dr. Daniel Steele, "to be holy in another, but to be holy in ourselves; not to be holy in our standing, but to be holy in our present state. In the nature of the case Christ can never be vicariously holy in our stead; vicarious suffering is possible, but vicarious character can have no existence save in man's imagination. The co-existence of a holy standing in Christ up in heaven, and an actual unholy state of character on earth, is a baseless illusion. The monstrous conception of a vicarious holiness is swept away by St. Peter's vigorous pen, 'Be ye, yourselves, also holy in all manner of living.' 1 Pet. i, 15." An imputed righteousness cannot be an inwrought righteousness. With the Arminian, faith means identification with Christ, laying hold upon Christ as that which the soul needs and must have. It means holding on to Christ at every sacrifice and against every temptation. It means, Every moment I have the witness of the Holy Spirit, that I am accepted of God through his well-beloved Son; that he is cleansing my soul, carrying on and up the great work of my eternal salvation, through my unreserved renunciation of all sin, my belief of the truth and exclusive dependence on the great atonement. "The chief want of the Calvinistic confessions of faith," says the earnest Calvinist, Dr. Newman Smythe, "is the play of the light and the hope of the Gospel over them." So long as Martin Luther entertained the view of faith Augustine taught he was chained in spiritual imbecility. But so soon as he obtained the true Lutheran faith, he became the monarch of the Reformation. "The Reformation," says Dr. Sprecher, "exposed the error and the defect of the previous methods of apprehending the doctrines of divine revelation, and in the light of justification by faith in Christ alone, it produced a complete change in the manner of apprehending the subject of personal salvation. To justifying faith the Scriptures present Christ as the central point of revealed truth." We thus see that the views of Bible theology which Calvinism imperatively necessitates differ, and necessarily must differ, fundamentally from those which the believer in a universal atonement is compelled to entertain.

If Paul were an Arminian, the Calvinist cannot possibly comprehend him, and if he were a Calvinian, the Arminian can never compass or fathom his system of faith and theology. If God foreordained the eternal destinies of all mankind, there must be nothing in theology or in Scripture exegesis inconsistent with that teaching. If he did not, there must be no interpretation inconsistent with the universality of the provisions for and the sincerity of the offer of eternal life to all. Predestination can never be reconciled with the notions of equity, righteousness and benevolence which the Scriptures so constantly advocate.

Between, "The just shall live by faith," and, "The just by faith, shall live," there is a wide distinction. No one can comprehend the apostle, who does not perceive that he means the just by faith, made just, regarded just, treated just by faith, shall live. The Bible, therefore, must remain a book of tantalizing enigmas, until these bodies of divines come to some general agreement. All, therefore, who devoutly love the holy Scriptures, will constantly feel the necessity of some new regulating principle of interpretation, some new ground upon which we all can meet, fraternize freely, and, seeing eye to eye, look down into the profundities and up into the sublimities of God's most holy word. In the very frequent surrenders, by learned Calvinistic commentators, of their most reliable texts, I see a manifest indication that on Calvinian foundations no scholarly theologian can ever construct a consistent Pauline theology. This any one could easily infer from the logical and practical weakness, darkness, and incertitude that necessarily attach to the Calvinistic views of those fundamental principles, which are so vehemently presented by St. Paul. It was never till Martin Luther lifted himself up from the Augustinian faith in objectivities, to the Lutheran faith in subjectivities, that he saw in celestial clearness the whole process of salvation. As long as he sought the forgiveness of sins by fastings and alms-giving and prayer, as expressly taught by St. Augustine, he found no relief, no peace to his soul. But as soon as he obtained the glorious thought of salvation by faith-alone in the blood of Jesus, which dawned upon him while studying the text, "If we confess our sins, he is faithful and just to forgive us our sins," his groans ceased, his agonies gave place to rapture and tears of gratitude. No wonder it was henceforth the one mission of his splendid life, to preach the great doctrine of salvation by faith alone in the blood of Jesus. Through this divine truth, this bright door, this opening into saving faith, he led the immortal

Wesley into unspeakable usefulness and ineffable glories.

When Isaac Newton climbed up into the moon and found universal gravitation nestling there, he caught such a view of his Maker as made him adore and obey him ever after. So when Martin Luther discovered the great law of spiritual attraction toward the mighty magnet resting on Calvary's cross, he obtained such a view of the Gospel, such an insight into the process of pardon and regeneration, as sent him flying over the earth with a message from eternity, as a seraph of light. This view ever after enraptured his soul, till he was carried by angels into the eternal sunshine of his Redeemer's presence on high.

Every Arminian knows that ever and anon he stumbles upon passages in the Bible that start his earnest inquiry, "How can I snatch that text out of the hands of the Calvinist, and yet maintain my reputation for scholarship and my character of candor?" These facts are disreputable to the commentators of the holy Scriptures. But so long as these two opposing systems of theology obtain, the Bible must remain an inexplicable and sealed book. Between its lines lie hallowed mysteries. But the absurdities which theologians and exegetes have crowded into its sacred lines must unceremoniously be swept therefrom. Nothing but divine nescience of future contingencies can ever eradicate the innumerable contradictions which commentators have crowded into that blessed book which God at such great cost has vouchsafed as a glorious revelation of himself, his thoughts and his purposes to his helpless, intelligent creatures. Only assume the truth of divine nescience, and a system of Scripture exegesis correspondent to our own instincts, intuitions, reason, conscience, experience, and consciousness, and our natural sense of things, runs throughout the entire holy volume with ever-increasing clearness. Without it the Bible remains, and must ever remain, full of inexplicable perplexities. Inertia makes astronomy the simplest of all the physical sciences. What inertia can do for astronomy, divine nescience can do for the Bible. In providence, and in all his great world-plans, God treats man as an instrument, and hence he puts the human will under the law of unconscious restraint and constraint. Relative to man's endless destiny God deals with him as a free agent, and hence his will is put under the law of liberty. Calvinians think that God treats man as an instrument not only in providence and in the great world-plans, but also in relation to his eternal state. Arminians think that God deals with man as an agent not only in reference to his everlasting destiny, but also in relation to the kingdom of providence and the great world-plans. But so long as the Bible is universally interpreted upon either of these false principles of hermeneutics, it must be a self-contradictory book, and retranslations shall be necessitated perpetually. The dualistic view of the human will, as being both an instrument and an agent, and the self-contradiction of foreknowing a future choice that either will be, or will not be, are the indispensable *desiderata* to a sound system of Bible hermeneutics. Divine nescience is the heliocentric place from which the apparent are the real motions of all the divine truths moving in the firmament of Revelation. Taking this doctrine as a stand-point, and assuming the dualistic action of the human will, light floods all the holy Scriptures. The Calvinist Froude says: "The Arminian has entangled the Calvinist, and the Calvinist has entangled the Arminian, in a labyrinth of contradictions, and therefore the crisis has uniformly been a drawn battle." Neither of them will surrender to the other principles he has so long urged as biblical truth. They may, however, consent to unite and agree upon some new criteria of interpretation which will work with lubricity through every perplexing text and difficult subject. In the interpretation of the holy Scriptures, manifestly a present uncertainty must not be regarded as a future certainty, a strong analogy between the divine and human intellects must not be denied; the dualistic action of the human will must be admitted, constrained when acting as an instrument, and free when acting as a free agent; the possibility of finite merit must not be questioned, and the ultimate reason for a rightness must be such as will make right as obligatory upon God as it is upon man. Without this ultimate ground of right Bible theology may be received upon the simple authority of demonstrated divine inspiration, but it never can be settled and systematized philosophically. And the latest writers upon morals confess that this ultimate ground of right has never yet been discovered. And so long as the volition of Deity enters even as an element in ultimate rightness, Scripture teachings on many fundamental subjects can never be philosophically defended.

But with the above indispensable principles of hermeneutics, a scholarly and spiritual exegesis can sweep all tantalizing perplexities out of the word of God.

It is mournful if not disreputable to the expounders of divine revelation that they have not furnished us with some comprehensive principles of interpretation that would exorcise from the holy Scriptures the unthinkables and the unbelievables that so appall the candid reader thereof, and compel him often to hesitate as to their divine origin.

Neither predestination, nor prescience, nor the narrowness of human comprehension, nor dissimilarity between the human and the divine intellects, nor God's independence of logical processes, nor the impossibility of succession of events with Deity, nor the eternal now, the timelessness of time, the durationlessness of duration, has ever been able to sweep babelic jargon from the word of the Lord, or to unlock to eager eyes and more eager hearts multitudes of its ineffable revelations. If we, therefore, from prejudice, or tenacity for old opinions, or partisan animus, or apprehension of lessened personal popularity, reject a hypothesis which, while diminishing none of the perfections of Deity, and necessitating no evils whatever, makes luminous with simplicity and directness the whole word of

God, before the final bar we never can be justified. We, therefore, fearlessly affirm that divine nescience of future contingencies is indispensable to a satisfactory interpretation of the holy Scriptures. "The harmony of any philosophy in itself is that which giveth to it light and evidence," said the immortal Francis Bacon.

CHAPTER X.

DIVINE NESCIENCE OF FUTURE CONTINGENCIES IS A NECESSITY TO AN EXPLANATION OF THE UTILITY OF PRAYER.

ATTEMPTS of the greatest minds and devoutest spirits, to explain the philosophy of prayer, have been numerous, herculean, but confessedly unsatisfactory, if not abortive. "When God turns aside the arrow from his praying child," says J. W. Alexander, "he does what he foresaw to be done from eternal ages." "Prayer," says Dr. C. Hodge, "has the same causal relation to the good bestowed as any means has to its end." But if the prayer be ordained how can it be causal to the good bestowed? "It is essential to the idea of mind-power that it should be free to act when, where and how it pleases," says Dr. Hodge. According to this, there can be no mind-power in prayer, for that prayer was sovereignly ordained by God. But if one is constrained to pray, as Dr. H. teaches, then one who does not pray is constrained to restrain prayer, and cast off the fear of God. If one who prays moves as he is moved upon, so does he move as he is moved upon who restrains prayer, because each feels the duty of prayer with equal imperativeness. How much less unreasonable the statement of a noted infidel that "the nature of this immense universality of things having been eternally adjusted, constituted and settled by the profound thought, perfect wisdom, impartial justice, immense goodness and omnipotent power of God, it is the greatest arrogance in us to attempt any alleviation thereof through prayer." If God has fore-ordained whatsoever comes to pass, your self-crimination for your neglect of the solemn duty of prayer would make Aristotle question your sanity or your sincerity or excite his gentlemanly mirthfulness over your illogical folly. " The prayer of the Calvinist," says S. Baring-Gould, " is as illogical as the prayer of the fatalist or the Mohammedan."

But to explicate the utility of prayer, under the pressure of the assumption of prescience of all future contingencies, would necessitate equally the dialectic scorn of the founder of logic. For if God foreknows all future contingencies, they now lie in his mind as immutable realities. They can be modified by no power short of the infinite. My prayers are either voluntary or they are involuntary. If they are involuntary, I am a machine, and liberty is impossible and necessity is unavoidable. If my prayers are voluntary, they may or they may not be presented before the throne of grace. But whether I pray or do not pray it cannot affect the cognition of which God is now perfectly conscious. But that which he now foreknows, one may reply, he foreknows as the result of what he foresees I will freely do. But suppose he does foreknow merely as the result of my voluntary prayer, still his present foreknowledge is subjectively infallible and objectively it is immutable. But if his foreknowledge is now infallible and immutable my voluntary prayer is absolutely inevitable. If my voluntary prayer is objectively inevitable, then there can be no conceivable grounds for me to be solicitous or to give myself the least uneasiness as to its actual performance. There is no possible need for me to bestir myself or distress myself or condemn myself on the subject of the discharge of this imperative and fundamental duty. There is no conceivable arena on which I can exercise my choice and put forth my volition. The logical and practical effect of my belief in divine foreknowledge is precisely the same on my faithfulness in the discharge of the duty of voluntary prayer as could be my belief in the eternal and unconditional decrees. I never can infract or modify that which God now infallibly foreknows. And this is true, though I am the arbiter of my own fate, the architect of my own immortal destiny. There stands God's immutable foreknowledge; my prayer or my non-prayer cannot change it in a solitary particular. I can no more affect that future reality which corresponds to divine foreknowledge than a babbling brook in its lisping murmuring could command the cataract of Niagara to check its rushing and plunging, and to cease forever its mighty thunderings.

I know I have not prayed enough in all the past, and that I have lost immeasurably in all my interests from my neglect of prayer. But, if absolute prescience be true, I have always prayed just as much and just as fervently as was exactly correspondent to the divine foreknowledge thereof which he has possessed from all eternity. Prayer means that God will do for a soul, on condition of its compliance with the duty of prayer, that which he will not do if that condition is not complied with. If the condition be complied with it effects changes in God, or prayer is a meaningless institution. If, from its purely human side, prayer can effect no real changes in the infinite mind and heart, it is an institution destitute of both sense and utility. But if prescience of contingencies be true, how can prayer exert the slightest influence in changing the thoughts, feelings, purposes and volitions of Deity? Upon the hypothesis of prescience, prayer can effect no changes in God. Thus one of the sublimest of all the sublime institutions of the Christian religion, one of the grandest of all the moral engines, stands forth before the world, not draped in the respectable habiliments of mystery, but in the disheartening garb of tantalizing absurdities. The truth is, that no theological thought or principle has yet been presented to Christendom that can light us on our way to the center of the philosophy of prayer. Philip Schaff says Richard Rothe is the greatest man Germany has produced since Schleiermacher, and he exclaims, "If absolute prescience be true, prayer becomes not only nonsense, but an inexcusable absurdity." But the simple principle of divine nescience of present nonentities of future contingencies bathes the whole subject of prayer, in all its profundities and heights, in all its comprehensiveness and power, in all its philosophies and results, and in all the wisdom of its adoption and blessedness of its efficiency, with an effulgence that satisfies the philosopher, soothes the believer, and inspires the pleader before the awful throne. It arrests the bending heavens, hails into immediate consciousness Father, Son, and Holy Ghost, and opens wide the hand filled with infinite benefactions, for all those who, renouncing all sin and relying exclusively upon the atonement, inquire of God "to do these things for them," and to whom he hath most graciously said, "While they are speaking I will hear."

A scientist who refuses to repudiate a principle that bothers him perpetually because it was taught him by a revered father, and rejects an hypothesis that works satisfactorily in every combination, will soon empty his lecture-room, and drop out of the eye of the devotee of science. And the student in theological mysteries who adopts similar procedures cannot reasonably hope long to escape a similar neglect and oblivion. Divine nescience of future contingencies is needed to make prayer reasonable, comprehensible, natural, real and completely effectual and all-prevailing.

CHAPTER XI.

DIVINE NESCIENCE OF FUTURE CONTINGENCIES IS NECESSARY TO THE CONSTRUCTION OF A VALUABLE THEODICY.

THE innumerable efforts of the greatest minds for hundreds of years to construct a satisfying theodicy prove how devout is the *desideratum*. A theodicy is a vindication of the perfection of God in establishing and permitting the order of things that from some cause obtains in this world. The word theodicy is derived from θεος, God, and δικη, justification. It does not propose to inquire, is God good or wise, just or powerful? but how the existence of sin came to pass, how suffering, injustice, oppression and misfortune can be explained without any criticism or reflection upon any of the divine attributes? The objections that must be met in a theodicy are the existence of moral evil, which is contrary to the holiness of God; the existence of physical evil, which is contrary to the goodness of God; the great disproportion between crimes and their punishments, the triumph of wickedness, the oppression of innocence, virtue and modest worth, which are contrary to the justice of God. Now, few are the problems in all the realms of thought, whose solution is more essential to our believing, determining, doing and rejoicing, as our nature and capacities clearly indicate we may and ought, than this very problem of the theodicy.

But what is this that I see, coming from Edom, with dyed garments from Bozrah, whose brightness is as the light adorned with the beauty of prophecy, arrayed in the splendor of miracles, traveling in the greatness of its strength, speaking in righteousness, covering the heavens with its glory, and filling the earth with its praise? and yet not one to be found among all its myriad devotees strong enough to loose the seal that locks a soul-satisfying theodicy. "The problem of evil," exclaims one, "is the knottiest of all the questions that ever perplexed the human mind." "The whole subject is one of inexplicable mystery. The origin of evil is an abyss in which the profoundest intellects are as completely beyond their depths as the most shallow," are the statements of Daniel Curry.

It would, indeed, be irreverent as well as foolish to attempt the construction of a theodicy without a fixed purpose to reject all self-contradictions from the discussions. Whenever two comprehensible propositions are incompatible with each other one or the other must always be rejected in any investigation. To incorporate an incompatibility into a theodicy, would be like introducing a minus in lieu of a plus, in the innumerable formulas needed in calculating the position, distance, size, orbit and perihelion, of an unknown planet, suspected of disturbing the *equilibria* of the solar system. Such incorporations of incompatibles has been the fatal defect and notorious defeat of all the theodicies yet proposed to the republic of thinkers. The source of weakness, confusion, and worthless results, will be found in the undue assumptions which the builders have regarded as necessities in themselves and indispensable to their schemes. Plato, for example, on the baseless fancy of the pre-existence of souls, tried in vain to account for present suffering and to justify the ways and dealings of divine Providence. Augustine, to explain these troublesome enigmas, invented and brought forward the disheartening scheme of predestination. He constructed his pitiless system out of inferences drawn from his reasonings on the single attribute of God's omnipotence, contemplated separately from other infinite perfections. John Calvin made God's will the originating cause of moral evil, and in this way he explained how evil could emanate from a pure creature. "The myriad-minded" Leibnitz brought one of the finest minds of the race, and bearing the largest resources of knowledge, to the elucidation of this ever-obtruding subject. He came to the construction of a satisfactory theodicy with a valor, self-reliance and confidence of ultimate success, that were truly sublime. But never in all the history of literature was there a failure more signal, more heralded, or more humbling to human pride. His system has been aptly described as a universe of shadows, or a mathematical romance. But how could it be otherwise, when he regarded and assumed that evil was an eternal necessity in the nature of things, over which God has no control? He laid the foundations of his theodicy on his inconceivable monads, his necessities of evils, his erroneous psychology, and his sadder misconceptions of theology and Bible truth.

To illumine this subject Albert Bledsoe built his explanation on the impossibility of creating a man free, and yet making it impossible for him to fall. Over the Calvinistic theodicy he fulminates with a hearty good-will. But the Calvinian in turn could let his logical lightning play about the head of Bledsoe with equal fury and reason. Bledsoe betrays a consciousness that there was a vulnerable point in his system. He manifests a half-formed conviction, that there was a quaking foundation for his idolized scheme. He utterly ruined his theodicy, the fruit of years of patient thought, when he made sin essential to the permanence and glory of the divine throne. "God," he says, "could have prevented moral evil by refusing to create those he foreknew would transgress his law, but he chose to create the world exactly as he did, though he foresaw the fall and all its consequences. He did this because he saw that the highest good of the universe required the creation of such a world." If this be true, then, sin really originated in infinite wisdom and benovelence, and is therefore an essential agency in the moral universe. But this is a conclusion too distressing and unreasonable for a moment's tolerance, in the evening of the nineteenth century.

But "it is a reproach to philosophy," said Dante, " to allow that the existence of moral evil is incomprehensible." The psychical and theological errors and the undue assumptions which have so long prevented the construction of a valid theodicy, ought diligently to be sought and promptly abandoned. "It is certain," said Bishop I. W. Wiley, who has read and thought widely upon such themes, "that the construction of a theodicy is utterly impossible on the basis of either the dogma of predestination or that of absolute prescience." And with this opinion every believer in either of these assumptions will very readily coincide. All hope of a theodicy must be abandoned, or some new principle of a construction must be discovered and agreed upon by theologians. But the hope of an acceptable theodicy is too important an achievement and too great a boon for the world ever to abandon its entertainment. No new principle has yet been presented for the consideration of patient inquirers after better and firmer foundations. Divine nescience of future contingencies is the thought that turns into gold every thing and every element needed in the construction of a splendid divine theodicy. In the light of this simple principle all those functions and factors, which hitherto have proved so troublesome to theodicists, lose all their mysteriousness. By its power we can transmute every one of them into a pure crystal to adorn the walls of our construction. It illumines the genesis of sin, explains the existence of evils, and accounts for all suffering. It dissipates the mysteriousness in the long triumph of injustice and in the afflictive dispensations of Heaven. It shows the causes of the slow progress of civilization, and the processes of such frequent relapses therein. It points out the origin of the imperfections of a divine and perfect religion, explains the causes of the hard-won victories of such a religion in a world that is perishing for the need of it. It pours floods of light over all the trials, perplexities, temptations, hardships, disappointments and responsibilities of human life. And so truly is this the case, that he who studies these hazards in the light of this hypothesis is not only serene beneath all his burdens, but, like St. Xavier, longs for "more, yet more," that his usefulness may be greater and his soul grander. May I not, then, confidently assert that divine nescience is a necessity to the construction of an acceptable theodicy, radiant with consistency and comfort? Divine nescience of future contingencies does for a theodicy what inertia does for the starry heavens. The simple truth that matter cannot change the state in which it is, is the principle that tunes the "music of the spheres" and maintains the harmonics and melodies all around the "milky way." And so divine nescience brings beauty, quietness, profit, and assurance forever into the great theodicean problem.

CHAPTER XII.

DIVINE NESCIENCE OF FUTURE CONTINGENCIES IS NECESSARY TO A UNIVERSAL ATONEMENT.

ABSOLUTE prescience coerces us, "*nolens volens,*" over a thousand texts of Holy Writ teaching the doctrine of an atonement that is universal, to the distressing dogmas of a limited atonement and a partial redemption of the human family. "The Lord hath laid on him the iniquity of us all," is the uniform testimony of the Old Testament Scriptures. "Jesus Christ by the grace of God hath tasted death for every man," is the unvarying declaration of the new covenant. The bottomless depths of these mysterious passages of God's holy Word we shall never be able fully to sound—certainly never in this life. But if they do not teach that I am individually under special obligations to the Redeemer, obligations too wide and high and deep for my present power of conception, then language is too imperfect an instrument, even in the hands of infinite wisdom, for any reliance in the communication of revealed thought. But that which Jesus Christ did for me individually, in his great work of atonement, he did for every other man in the wide, wide world. If there was any suffering, humiliation, commiseration; if there was any dying love, any thing hard to surrender or terrible to endure in the depths of the great atoning sacrifice of Jesus Christ on the cross; if there was any significance in the spikes, the spear, the scoffs, the thorns, the vinegar, and the hiding of his Father's face, it was all endured for each and for every soul of man. Jesus made for every man ample provision for the pardon of all his guilt. He made it possible for him to exchange a demon nature for an angelic one. He restored to him the forfeited power of alternative choices. He incipiently regenerated his soul up to the point that would make it possible for him to perceive, to hear, to feel and to embrace the great salvation. And, besides all this, he purchased for him the extraordinary influence of the Holy Ghost in a plenitude greater than was vouchsafed even to unfallen Adam. "Jesus Christ by the grace of God tasted death for every man." This means that he suffered for every individual of the race as specifically and individually as though he died for each alone. All the elements involved in a sacrificial death for a specified man were involved in the propitiation Jesus made for the whole world. Through an atonement he could not have procured for a single person more benefits or privileges, nor could he have advanced any higher claims upon his personal gratitude and obedience, than he did for every individual of the race. If any man on earth has any spiritual deliverance or any gracious privilege it is only through the sacrificial sufferings of Jesus Christ. But where could be the wisdom or the righteousness, justice or propriety, of making such costly provisions, reaching to such innumerable particulars, effecting such moral changes in nature and relations to the Infinite for the whole race, and also satisfying infinite justice for all men, when it was certain that all such provisions and satisfactions would never be availed of or improved or embraced by a portion of the human family? Why undergo the agonies of the crucifixion, why meet the powers of the violated law, why pass into those mysterious shadows exclaiming, "My God, my God, why hast thou forsaken me?" for all those foreknown to be incorrigible reprobates? How needless and wasteful for the Redeemer to groan in atoning, to travail in the bitterness of his soul, and to implore in the depths of his pity for the salvation of one foreknown to be a vessel of wrath fitted only for destruction? What father could provide a library for an idiotic son, or a throne for an insane one? And could the Redeemer be less wise to provide a throne in heaven for one foreknown to be an outcast, and to be bound in everlasting chains? But such excruciating provisions were not only unwise and useless, there was in them really a refinement of cruelty. Christ, in making a propitiation for the sins of the world, placed upon the incorrigible unspeakable obligations which he knew would be wholly disregarded, thus intensifying the darkness of their eternal night.

The Westminster Confession of Faith says, "Neither are any other redeemed by Christ, effectually called, justified, adopted, sanctified or saved but the elect only." The late Dean Stanley, that prodigy of sweet spirit and elegant diction, commenting upon this passage of the Confession, says: " Looking calmly upon this statement, it is hardly possibly to conceive that the doctrine it contains, however crudely expressed, could be objected to by any human being." The most excellent Dean had a strange frailty in leaning leniently toward many fundamental religious errors. But in this case he was as logical as Aristotle himself. His penetrating eye saw that the assumption of absolute prescience necessitated the truth of a limited atonement. This earth has already passed through very many epochs, ever emerging, however, from a state less perfect into one more perfect, with more beauty of form and for the accomplishment of higher ends. New developments and new eras and new missions await in the future history of our globe. Innumerable epochs may lie in the far-reaching world-plans of Jehovah. It is certain the holy Scripture prophesies of a state in which the order of things will be entirely dissimilar to that order which now obtains in the earth. We know with what precision and accuracy God adjusts his creations. Even if a pebble should drop into annihilation out of the solar system, astronomers tell us, nothing but the interference of an omnipotent hand could counteract the influence of its loss and preserve in *equilibria* the disturbed and rocking celestial systems. And so, doubtless, in the creation of the human race he resolved upon the exact number of immortal souls who should take their incipiency in a human body " wonderfully and fearfully made." This precise number may have had important relations to other parts of his great temporal plans. For each one of this precise number of deathless souls the great Redeemer did or did not suffer and die. The commercial view of the atonement is, that the atonement was a literal payment of a debt, and, therefore, it must be a limited atonement. The United Synod of Scotland said: "Many assert that Christ made atonement for all men, and thus infringe the sovereignty of divine grace and encourage the presumption of the sinner; therefore the synod enjoins all its ministers to be on their guard against introducing discussions or employing language which may seem to oppose the doctrine of a particular redemption, or that Christ in making an atonement for sin was substituted in the room of the elect only, and which may unsettle the minds of the people on this point or give occasion to members of the Church to suspect the purity of our faith." Dr. Cairns, of Scotland, in the recent Pan-Presbyterian Alliance, said, "In the sense of ultimate salvation, none are redeemed by Christ but the elect only." Dr. Miley, one of the soundest and broadest of living Arminians, and author of a most valuable work on the atonement in Christ, said to me: "To harmonize the doctrine of absolute prescience with the universality of the atonement is a difficulty I have never yet penetrated; it is an enigma I have never been able to solve." "I see not now," said Bishop Wiley, "how we can possibly escape a limited atonement if absolute prescience be assumed." But a limited atonement robs the Bible of one of its transcendent glories, a universal atonement in Jesus Christ. To rob the world of such a fact and such a thought would fill it with anguish and dismay which nothing could ever alleviate. How infinitely painful the consideration of such a thought! Every true minister of Christ preaching salvation to perishing congregations would grow ghastly or petrified lest he might be addressing some poor immortal child for whose salvation no provision had ever been actually made. The sorrow, the sighing, the unutterable oppression over the announcement of only a limited atonement for the human race would not be confined to this mundane sphere.

Angels would sympathize, weep, be silent and wonder-smitten, over the unspeakable woe and merciless reality. But, millions on millions of thanks be given to Jesus Christ, the adorable Redeemer of the human family, a limited atonement is not true. It is alike unreasonable and unscriptural. It is too horrible for conception, and much more for utterance. It is an unmitigated slander on God's holy Word. It is a blasphemous reflection upon the value of Christ's death, upon the efficiency of the Holy Ghost, and the sincerity of God in offering life to all mankind.

But with the establishment of the doctrine of a universal atonement absolute prescience is demonstrated to be utterly untenable.

Divine nescience of future contingencies establishes, firm as the heavens, the truth of an unlimited atonement made by him who "was a propitiation for the sins of the whole world."

Prescience affirms necessity, champions pantheism, paralyzes prayer, annihilates the sanctions of endless retributions; but we now see that it braves anathemas, in denying that the glorious atonement was ever intended for the whole world.

CHAPTER XIII.

BUT DIVINE NESCIENCE OF FUTURE CONTINGENCIES IS A NECESSITY IN ITS FAR-REACHING RELATIONS TO ANOTHER IMPORTANT DOCTRINE OF DIVINE REVELATION.

THE doctrine of the endless separation of the wicked from the essential presence of God, in a state of conscious degradation and loss, has been more unfortunately presented than any other Bible tenet. Its opponents and adherents have been equally unfortunate in their statements of the proposition. These shocking misrepresentations of the revealed truth have wrought enervation in the Church and wide-spread deception and ruin to souls. The evils that have been wrought in this way all along the ages transcend the power of angelic computation. "The world," said Jonathan Edwards, "will be converted into a great lake of liquid fire, in which the wicked shall be overwhelmed, which shall always be in tempest, in which they shall be tossed to and fro, having no rest day nor night, vast billows of fire continually rolling over their heads, of which they shall ever be full of a quick sense, within and without; their heads, their eyes, their tongues, their hands, their feet, their loins and their vitals shall ever be full of a glowing, melting fire, enough to melt the very rocks and elements. Also they shall be full of the most quick and lively sense to feel the torments, not for ten millions of ages, but for ever and ever, without any end at all." Such presentations of the endless wretchedness of the incorrigible really seem based on fiendish vengeance. They are so inconsistent with our intuitive conceptions of the goodness of God that we instinctively inquire whether such a doctrine can possibly be found among divine revelations.

As to the condition of the incorrigible after death, the first question is, Will they be annihilated? If the hypothesis of annihilation be true, it is one of the most important of all subordinate truths. It ought to be blazoned on the heavens and seen of all ages, and yet it is not even suggested by Him who taught as man never taught. On the endless suffering of the wicked he gives frequent and most impressive lessons, but on their annihilation he is absolutely silent. The word αιων, which he uses to express the eternity of the Deity and the unending blessedness of the righteous, he employs to describe the changeless condition, the irreversible existence, of the incorrigible. A message from the Infinite to the finite must contain a largeness of signification which it is impossible for any finite messenger fully to comprehend. None but the Infinite himself can so fully comprehend his own truth as to express it infallibly. Jesus, being Infinite, fully comprehended his own teaching. And this word αιων is the word he uses to express the endless future of the wicked.

Those who were personally addressed by our Lord never dreamed that he taught the doctrine of the annihilation of the wicked. If it had been his purpose to teach the doctrine of endless punishment he could not have found a word more perfect to express his meaning. No word in the Greek language so fully and so perfectly expresses duration without any limitation as this word αιων. It is derived from that root whose complete formation is the adverb αὲι, forever. To αὲι we trace the English ever, the German *ewig*, the Latin *æternitas*, and our word eternity. Aristotle, believing the heavens were eternal, regarded them as the measure of eternity ; and he uses the word αιων to express the full period which includes the existence of the heavens, and the existence of all things past and future, the existence of the infinite itself, and also the existence of infinite duration. Plato, believing that the heavens, were created and not eternal, contrasts them with αιων, saying that long-enduring as are the heavens, they are the measures of time, while αιων is absolutely without measure or movement or change. " The wicked," says our Lord, " shall go away into everlasting punishment." Κόλασις, the word translated punishment, does not mean annihilation, but suffering. It is not even tinged with the notion of annihilation. If Jesus does not assert the endless suffering of the wicked, he does not affirm the endless happiness of the righteous. And thus he has always been understood through all the ages of the Christian era. All uncritical readers, and ninety-nine out of every hundred who have critically studied Christ's discourses for two thousand years, have believed that he clearly taught the endless separation of the wicked from the righteous in a state of conscious existence.

If the doctrine of annihilation be true Jesus fully believed it; and if he did believe it, he made carefully studied efforts to conceal his real sentiments and convictions upon the subject. But he who came into the world to bear witness to the truth could never practice such unworthy concealments. And to show that Jesus taught the annihilation of the wicked is a task too herculean even for an army of biblical critics. Indeed, it is difficult to see how God could have made the doctrine of endless separation from himself in conscious existence of incorrigible souls any plainer than it is presented in the holy Scriptures, without abandoning what Bishop Butler calls his chosen method of revealed instruction, which is not to make revelations so overwhelming as to *coerce* the belief of free agents. Certainly no other doctrine of the Bible is stated more clearly or more impressively. If a torturing exegesis can pluck this teaching from revelation it can explain into insignificance any other of God's expressed thoughts.

"When I find," says Bishop Foster, in his "Beyond the Grave," that book of brilliancy and power, "the doctrine of future punishment omnipresent in the whole scheme, from beginning to end, of the holy volume, an underlying cardinal implication throughout and expressly stated many times, I am compelled to give in my adhesion. The Book masters me as an authority. I cannot reject it. I have no skill to torture any other meaning out of its language." Even Canon Farrar, who exclaims, " I am no Universalist," is compelled to say that the affirmation of annihilation greatly distorts the holy Scriptures. Two facts are manifest. God has in innumerable instances declared that the existence of the wicked shall be endless, and, secondly, he has nowhere hinted that he intends their annihilation. Why he cannot or why he will not annihilate the wicked he has not seen proper to reveal to us, and of this we have no right to complain. It may be that he could not do it without graver evils resulting to his other empires. It is possible that the annihilation of the disobedient would utterly prevent any such thing as a probation at all. For in the absence of an atonement, annihilation must needs follow immediately on the occasion of any willful violation of God's law. Because continuance in existence would only be to multiply violations and perpetrate further evils and examples to the moral universe. For an intelligent being to treat a God-given existence with such infinite contempt as deliberately to prefer annihilation to the endless, blissful fellowship with his glorious Creator, may be a sin whose depth only the eye of the infinite could ever penetrate. A transgression of God's moral law becomes a fact which he can neither annihilate nor render oblivious to his intelligent universe. Holy deeds are followed necessarily by an endless succession of benign influences. To interfere and prevent such necessary results would be an abandonment of fundamental governmental principles in both the nature of things and in the purposes of the Sovereign Ruler. So, in like manner, the nature of things, the purposes of God and the interests of the moral universe all require that deeds of wickedness be followed by an endless succession of disadvantages and depreciating influences, as illustrious warnings to all in probationary states. He who voluntarily sins introduces into the historic universe a new cause, prolific of evils, which must work its corrupting effects forever. As the evil effects of this newly created cause must be endless, so, in like manner, the manifestation of the divine displeasure must also be endless. God owes it to his moral universe to counteract, as far as possible, the evils of sin, and to repair the damage and defeat wrought by the sinner. A temporary divine displeasure toward him, while the damaging results of his wickedness continue to be endless, would necessitate remediless injury to his moral government. For any procedure that could dim or diminish or question the certainty of the divine displeasure toward sin would be an unspeakable calamity. The necessity, therefore, of the eternity of the divine displeasure toward sin absolutely prohibits the annihilation of the wicked person who originated that sin and inaugurated its baleful effects. Innumerable evils, all inconceivable to us, might result to this world and all worlds from the enactment of such a statute as the annihilation of the disobedient. But, doubtless, there are factors involved in this subject beyond our knowledge or even our power to conceive. "The idea," says Bishop Foster, "of the endless conscious suffering of the wicked is the most unwelcome thought ever suggested to my mind. My whole soul revolts against it. There is no sacrifice I would not willingly make to get rid of it. It is the horror of all horrors. Such is the attitude of my mind to the question. But, against my wish and all the feelings of my soul, I am constrained to believe that God sees it differently, and with infinitely greater capacity to know what is best and proper, and with infinitely greater love and tenderness than any of his holiest children can claim, has incorporated the dreadful fact of permanent conscious suffering as a possibility in his plan. For some cause too deep for my comprehension he will allow souls to live forever that will not be happy, and to whom existence will be perpetual ' shame and everlasting contempt.' I do not now see either wisdom or goodness in the plan, and possibly never may; I even doubt if I ever shall; but my faith and confidence are not measured by my power of comprehension."

No doubt the annihilation of the wicked would take place and its announcement would be made in divine revelation if immutable rightness and the welfare of the moral universe did not present an abatis of opposing moral considerations if not of self-contradictions. For any teacher, therefore, sent of God, to inculcate the doctrine of annihilation without the slightest intimation of its truth from the teachings of divine revelation, is certainly a hazard too frightful to contemplate. But a proper statement of eschatology hitherto has been impossible on account of our ignorance of the ultimate ground of right. A clear apprehension of that ground would conduct us directly to the heart of the subject and open it up to us in all its reasonableness and deep necessities. All philosophers up to this time agree that the ultimate ground of right has not been reached.

Unless there be an uncaused Creator of all things, all philosophical thinking must be barren of any valuable results. The recognition of the existence of Deity is necessary to all logical thought. We, therefore, say that God exists of necessity. He must possess all perfections and be destitute of every conceivable imperfection. "Our whole nature," says Bishop Butler, "leads us to conclude that God's will and character must be morally just and good, and we cannot even in imagination conceive it to be otherwise." But while God exists from necessity, he does not act from necessity. Freedom is one of the essential perfections of Deity. If he is free he can volitionate concordantly or discordantly with the standard of excellences which are concreted in his necessary existence. "This possibility," says the Calvinian, Mark Hopkins, "must necessarily be allowed as a mental conceivability." God cannot volitionate in opposition to this absolute standard of excellence, and continue or preserve his absolute perfection. But if he continues to volitionate in harmony with that standard he will forever preserve in volitional perfection the absolute perfection that from eternity existed of necessity. To maintain the perfections of his nature, and to achieve absolute rectitude, he must ever volitionate in harmony with the absolutely perfect standard. He has no more right nor liberty to depart from that standard than I have. Absolute rectitude is the result of a perfect being volitionating in harmony with the absolute perfections of Deity as they existed from eternity and of necessity. The abstract quality of rectitude is immutable rightness. Immutable rightness, then, is the quality that is concreted into absolute rectitude. "Every philosophy and philosopher," says S. Baring-Gould, "has failed to find an immutable principle of right which is of universal application."

But after the foregoing definitions of necessary self-existent perfection in nature, and of volitional absolute rectitude in the concrete Infinite, and of rightness, the abstract quality involved in absolute volitional rectitude, we need no longer nor deeper search for the immovable foundations of rightness, and the immutable principle of right, which is of universal application. To reach these ultimate principles, we need only to distinguish between the existence of infinite perfections and the free exercise of those perfections.

Rightness, therefore, is an intellectuality and an objectivity; it is neither a subjectivity nor a sensibility. It is instinctively perceived by all moral beings, and is perceived to be essential to the preservation of all kinds of excellence. Its perception is a necessity to accountability.

Right is intuitive and necessary, depending upon no will, but obligating all wills. Ultimate rightness, therefore, cannot rest on the arbitrary will of God. God is compelled to submit to the objective claims of immutable rightness, if he would preserve his own absolute excellence and achieve absolute rectitude. The perfection of the universe required the creation of accountable beings. But if God create free beings, he must not coerce their free wills. He cannot control the free in actions that are rewardable or punishable. Moral character is the result of freely volitionating in harmony with the standard of immutable rightness. An immoral character is the result of freely volitionating in opposition to that standard. God cannot create a moral character for one free agent, nor can he prevent another free agent from creating an immoral character for himself. God cannot prevent a good character from enriching and ennobling and emparadising the nature of its subject. Nor could he prevent an immoral character from degrading and distressing that nature. He could no more do this than he could make sin a blessing, or wrong to be right, or light to be darkness. He cannot force a free being to love him nor prevent a bad free being from hating him. Degradation, guilt, remorse, loss of self-respect, shame, weakness, unhappiness, and detestation of all holy beings, and the utter disqualification to enjoy God, flow inevitably from willful violation of immutable rightness. Every additional violation adds additional weakness to the conscience, darkness to the mind, hardness to the heart and perverseness to the will. In this process the soul finally reaches a state in which it is irredeemably fixed in its awfully shocking depravities. Observation, as well as philosophy, teaches us that persistence in wickedness tends to a state of being morally petrified.

"Whatsoever a man soweth that shall he also reap. He that soweth to the flesh shall of the flesh reap corruption." These are the terrible announcements of infallible truth. Incorrigibility results from persistent volitionating in opposition to rightness, to the dictates of reason, and the monitions of conscience, until no susceptibility remains in the soul which could ever respond to the attractions of obedience and the delights of holiness. When the soul is thus thoroughly ruined it possesses no recuperative power by which it can stir itself to the task of self-reformation. The elements of soul-regeneration are completely and forever exhausted. No thinker questions but that persistency in sin tends to endless fixity in moral nature. Prolonged dissimilarity of feeling with God ends necessarily in endless dissimilarity with him. None of his glorious perfections can ever be incorporated in such a degraded nature. From such a nature all the glorious endowments and possibilities have perished forever. The habits of disobedience deliberately fixed and settled, the incorrigibleness of a perverse will and the calloused, indurated sensibilities formed in the present state of gracious probation render worthless any future dispensations of mercy, hopeless to Deity, and useless to the lost soul.

No man would improve the present probation if one in the future were assured him. A promise of a future opportunity would be his charter for recklessness in this. If the present is misimproved its misimprovement will de-energize the soul of all those moral energies indispensable for entrance upon a future probation. Sin stupefies the moral sense; viciousness makes the soul insensible to appeal and impervious to light. "The wicked are held by the cords of their sins," says the wise man. There is a dreadful coercion in our iniquities. "From the wicked," says Job, "their light is withdrawn." To the incorrigible, even here, God says, let him alone, he is joined to his idols. The impenitent soul would enter eternity rifled of its susceptibilities, demonized by its habits, and blasted in its whole nature. What ground of hope, then, can we have that a soul incorrigible here would seek the path of obedience there? He will find no more light, and no greater considerations for virtue there than he has here. Men see and feel the terrible consequences of sin in this life, but still persist in wickedness. They regret their indulgence in sinful gratifications, but sin on as with a cart rope. The ancients had our three-score-years-and-ten probation, a dozen times repeated, but, notwithstanding all, they persevered in wickedness to the bitter end; and to-day nothing is so welcome to the unholy as the flimsy hypothesis of a future probation. This groundless hope grants them license to indulge in unholy living now, and awakens in them a hope of reformation hereafter. But what ground is there for the belief that they will initiate holiness in a future state of probation? Any number of future states of probation could never be availing to restore to an incorrigible soul its lost moral capacities. There is nothing in mere consequential endurance of the wretchedness inseparable from wickedness to incorporate into the soul any love of holiness for itself, or any purpose of praiseworthy obedience, or any desire for those qualifications needed to enjoy God and the society of saints. Suffering may subdue obstinacy, but it cannot restore lost susceptibilities, or lift out of moral degradation, or transform a fiend into an angel of light. Where is the basis of hope when depravity has penetrated and pervaded every vein, nerve and fiber of the soul? How can the agonies of depravity root out depravity and repugnance to holiness?

No motives can be presented there greater than the motives presented here. Jesus clearly teaches that probationers are more likely to hear Moses and the prophets than they would any preacher commissioned from perdition. But the Bible nowhere hints that perdition is a probation. Suffering cannot recreate the soul in righteousness and true holiness. A second probation assumes that pain is more efficacious in the regeneration of a depraved soul than the unsearchable riches and resources of the Son of God, and the mysterious powers of the Holy Ghost in changing from glory to glory. If suffering could transform the fallen soul, the incarnation were needless and all the refining processes of the Holy Ghost could be dispensed with. But neither the bitterness of disobedience nor the indescribable woes of depravity can ever regenerate and sanctify a child of Satan. The problem of all the ages has been to exorcise wickedness out of a disobedient soul. The soul saturated in iniquity cannot stir itself to delight in any thing good or holy. Death can effect no changes in the moral nature of the incorrigible. There is no possibility of his ever freely choosing to achieve a moral character, after his nature has been fixed in a state of vehement wickedness and aversion to holiness and obedience. The conditions which render the achievement of moral character possible can never exist hereafter. There will be no possibility in the fathomless depths of the depravity of a lost soul for the choice of a loving, reverent obedience beyond the grave. Any theater where vice has not attractions and virtue difficulties, could not afford a legitimate arena for the achievement of moral character. A mere wish to escape suffering and despair furnishes no opportunity whatever for a choice between the attractions of vice and the difficulties of virtue, that could in any way or degree be creative of moral excellence and rewardability. The lost soul is incapable of any feeling but a desire to escape pain. It cannot desire truth, goodness, love, nor God.

There is absolutely nothing in the soul of the lost that can ever respond to true holiness. Sin could never be forgiven until repented of. But even if there were something in the lost soul responsive to divine mandates and inclined to repentance, what evidence have we that the grace of repentance will be vouchsafed to the finally impenitent.

Men cannot repent, even in this life, without the grace of repentance being given to them by the Holy Ghost. It requires the persistent efforts of the Holy Ghost to bring any soul to the work of reformation. But has the lost soul the energies of the Holy Ghost to aid him in his most difficult work of penitence? Does the Holy Ghost, ignoring the awful declarations of Scripture that there is a sin unto death, and that the sin against himself can never be forgiven in this world nor in the world to come, continue his beseechings in the ears of the incorrigible in the place prepared for the devil and angels? God said to the inhabitants of the earth, "My spirit shall not always strive with man." Will he change his procedure in hell? But is the gospel of recovery preached in perdition?

There is a passage in the Epistle of Peter that has been thought to support such an affirmation: "It is better that ye suffer for well-doing than for evil-doing. For Christ also suffered once for all for sins, the just for the unjust, that he might bring us to God, having been put to death in the flesh, but having been quickened by the Spirit, in which also he went and preached unto the spirits in prison, having been disobedient aforetime (not were disobedient) when the long-suffering of God waited in the days of Noah. Forasmuch then as Christ hath suffered for us in the flesh, arm yourselves likewise with the same mind, for he that hath suffered in the flesh hath ceased from sin, that ye may live no longer to the lusts of men but to the will of God." One of the favorite studies of St. Peter was the writings of his brother Paul, in which he found many things difficult for him to comprehend. But he discovered that Paul had, humanly speaking, clearer conceptions of the deep spirituality of Christianity than any other one of the apostles. True, whatever any of the apostles uttered and presented as inspired was infallible, nevertheless they were strongly inclined to lay the foundation of the Church in the faith of Israel. Paul, however, had breadth enough to found a universal and permanent religion on Jesus Christ as chief corner-stone elect and precious. Peter, observing this depth of meaning in the preaching of St. Paul, was deeply imbued with its spirit and thought. Paul had taught the Romans that Jesus Christ according to the flesh was born of the seed of David, but was demonstrated to be the Son of God by the power of the Holy Ghost in the splendid fact of his resurrection from the dead. In penning the passage under consideration, I think Peter had in his memory this teaching of Paul. When the Scriptures wish to speak of the putting forth of observed divine energy and power, they use the term Spirit of God. For example, it is said, "Ye shall receive power, the Holy Ghost coming upon you." "God anointed

Jesus with the Holy Ghost and with power." Jesus, having suffered even unto death, was elevated to glory by the Holy Ghost. In the Epistle of Peter four great thoughts seem to be constantly struggling for utterance. They tinge all trains of his meditations. These thoughts to which he makes such constant reference are, the sufferings of Christ, the power of the Holy Ghost, the spirituality of the Church, and the condition of the lost. In the passage above quoted he tells the Church, exposed to persecution on all sides, it is better to suffer for well-doing than to suffer for ill-doing. This thought he impresses by the example of Christ, the greatest of all sufferers. The suffering of the Church for righteousness' sake suggests to his mind the suffering of the Redeemer for a lost and ruined world. The sufferings and death of the Saviour suggest his triumphant resurrection through the power of the Holy Ghost. The quickening, raising of Christ from the dead, naturally suggests his powerful manifestation under the preaching of the Gospel. The glorious manifestations of the Holy Ghost through the preaching of the apostles, bringing from darkness to light three thousand in a day, naturally suggests the smallness of his success under the preaching of Noah, that great preacher of righteousness, saving only eight souls out of an innumerable host through a period protracted for a hundred and twenty years. The antediluvians were notorious in Jewish history for their persistency of wickedness. They continued in this wickedness, says the Saviour, until the very day that

Noah entered into the ark and the flood came and destroyed them all. The almost utter failure of the Holy Ghost in saving the antediluvians would naturally suggest to Peter the multitudes of the finally lost. In meditating upon those unnumbered multitudes, the place of their present abode would necessarily be suggested to his feeling heart. But there is nothing in the train of thought or in the connection that could naturally or logically suggest the descent of Jesus into the lower world, or into the place prepared for the devil and his angels, to re-open the doors of invitation and hope. The thought of such a descent is wholly foreign to the mind of Peter, and it is grammatically impossible to the Greek text. In the examination of 1 Peter iii, 19 and 20, two inquiries force themselves upon our attention: Did the disobedience that is spoken of, take place at the time of the preaching that is spoken of; or was the preaching at one time and the disobedience at another time? Were these two events co-existent, synchronous, or were they not? If the Greek language has not resources sufficient to answer these questions it would be an instance of its imperfection. If that language can determine these questions, it would be an imperfection in Greek scholarship not to perceive and know it. In the Greek language, a participle agreeing with a noun expresses an essential attribute of that noun, provided both the noun and the participle have the article.

But if the noun has the article and the participle agreeing with it has not the article, then the participle expresses not an essential attribute of the noun, but some accidental circumstance of the noun. Our authorized version as well as the new translation translates the participle απειθησασι as a finite verb with a relative pronoun, " who were disobedient." This translation would be correct if the participle were preceded by the article τοις. If the article were present the participle would express the absolute general and habitual disobedience of the antediluvians to all God's mandates, and it would not necessitate the co-existence of the two events. But if the article were not before the participle, then the participle would express the specific disobedience of the antediluvians to the specific preaching addressed to them. This would necessitate the co-existence of the disobedience and the preaching. The aorist participle απειθησασι being without the article τοις, and referring back to the noun πνευμασι, which has the article, expresses not an essential attribute, but merely a contingent circumstance of the noun. Indeed, the participle has the sense of an adjective, and implies that the disobedience spoken of was co-existent with the preaching spoken of. It really describes the disobedient state of the spirits at the time of Noah, and under his preaching. This aorist participle, therefore, being without the article, demonstrates that the preaching spoken of and the disobedience of the spirits were synchronous events. And this demonstrates that the preaching spoken of was not performed by Christ, but by Noah under the special call and inspiration of the Holy

Ghost, who also strove mightily with the people of that generation. The rendering of this participle by a finite verb with the relative pronoun, is not allowed by the Greek language. There is, therefore, no basis for the hypothesis of Christ's preaching his Gospel to the antediluvians in the under world or in the abode of the lost. Besides the grammatical prohibition of this rendering, nothing could have been more irrelevant in the logical train of St. Peter's thoughts, than the going of Christ between his death and resurrection to offer to the lost, deliverance from the great calamity of sin. We thus see that there is no countenance given in the Scriptures to the hypothesis of a future probationary state. They uniformly represent the condition of the finally impenitent as a state forever irreversible.

But all this discussion is upon the hypothesis that the incorrigible possess the power of contrary choice. This hypothesis is, however, a groundless assumption. As soon as man sinned his will dropped from the law of liberty down to the law of cause and effect. Jesus was promised, and he restored to the will its lost power of contrary choice, its original freedom. This gracious power is vouchsafed to us through our probationary existence. If this power is used in choosing rebellion it will be forever withdrawn, and the being remains under the chains of necessity, forever bereft of all power of alternate choices.

Without an atonement restoration to the divine favor, after the fall, would have been impossible.

This is unquestionable, if moral law has any signification or imperativeness, or if moral government urges any inexorable requisitions necessary to the weal of the universe. If restoration to the divine likeness and favor were impossible without an atoning sacrifice, it was because the will was incapable of choosing repentance and obedience. If the soul was incapable of choosing reformation, it was because the power of alternative choices was taken from it in its disobedience. This power of alternative choices, which was lost on the probation of works, was purchased back for man by the Redeemer. But if it be lost a second time, on the second great probation under a remedial dispensation of mercy and faith, then both revelation and reason inform, that it can never be restored or proffered through future probations. For moral government demands, and must demand, final settlements and adjudications with its moral subjects. If these settlements are indefinitely deferred through interminable probations, moral government must necessarily lose its signification, surrender its restraints, tear away its majestic imperiousness, undermine the foundations of the eternal throne, shatter the confidence of loyal millions, and wholly misrepresent its arbiter. There must, therefore, be a point in probation beyond which the power of alternative choices cannot be continued. At this point right, righteousness, justice, good government and the welfare of all worlds imperatively require that freedom be taken from the incorrigible. When this point has been reached the free-will ceases to be a free-will, and falls into the plane of a constrained will. The fact that neither Satan, nor any who followed his lead into ruin, have ever returned to obedience and happiness and heaven, is overwhelming proof that their wills are now no longer free to choose happiness, but are constrained to act as by fate. If there is eternal hope, why has not some one of those who are suffering the vengeance of eternal fire been released, and, clad in angel robes, ascended to God's right hand? If there is eternal hope, why has not Satan climbed back into paradise? How mournful the vision of a soul bereft of its freedom! How grand, how splendid was Satan ere he lost his liberty and was bound in everlasting chains! For what high resolves was he once capacitated! What magnificent purposes, he once had power to perform! Once he could say, " I will fathom the mysteries of the divine nature. I will soar up into the seventh heaven of moral purity. I will compass the outmost limits of my divinely-spoken destiny. I will lay out comprehensive plans, for carrying on the moral development of all worlds. I will travel through the universe, and quaff from all fountains sacred, high eternal joys. I will live forever in the presence of the Lord of hosts, rejoicing in his favor and illustrating his perfections." But now how changed! He cannot now *choose* the right, the just, the good, the beautiful, the glorious. As easily could *I* speak a new world into existence, and send it revolving into the heavens, as Satan could make the feeblest resolve in the direction of obedience or of benevolence. In him that godlike faculty has perished, and his once great and splendid soul stands forth to-day in monumental ruins, clothed in moral darkness and melancholy gloom, visible to all intelligent worlds, and paining God forever.

Thus we see that sound philosophy adds its testimony to that of inspiration, that a great gulf is necessarily fixed between the saved and the lost, the righteous and the unrighteous. Over this gulf there is no passage for saint or sinner world without end. There will be no possibility for the choice of a loving obedience beyond the present life. This is the inevitable consequence of incorrigibility. Even if God could prevent sin from degrading the soul, there could be no moral certainties any where in the moral universe. All would be eternal suspense and unutterable uncertainty. Better a thousand times annul gravitation and allow all material worlds to rush into conglomerate ruin, than to annul the indissoluble connection between wickedness and woe. Such a procedure could not fail to fill heaven, to fill the universe, and to all eternity, with night, chaos and despair. "If the light in us becomes darkness, how great is that darkness?" inquires our Lord. The question now arises, Are these inevitable consequences of sin to be regarded as divine penalties? Penalty is suffering inflicted by rightful authority for the violation of law. God does inflict penalties upon individuals and nations. He does this for punishment, for discipline, for correction, and for example for the warning of others. He does this to subserve his temporary purposes, and his great world-plans. But all such penalties are merely reformatory. They imply a capacity of improvement in those who are exercised thereby. But beyond the natural consequences of wickedness, there are no penalties beyond the grave. After probation, God never punishes a soul. He does not inflict endless penalties upon the incorrigible. They inflict them upon themselves. The punishment of the disobedient is the mere working out of natural and necessary law. Hell is the inevitable result of persistent wickedness. Banishment from God, is the necessary consequence of soul degradation. If a man is bad, he is miserable and degraded, without any wish or efficiency or interference of Deity entering into that wretchedness. The consequences of disobedience do not flow from the divine wish or the divine arrangement, but from the deep necessities of the nature of the case. Into the endless curses of sin not a single element of divine volition or of divine satisfaction can ever enter. That God is gratified over the agonies of ruined souls is self-contradictory. There is not a sting in the suffering of the lost, God ever voluntarily put there. The eternal consequences of sin, is not the dogma of divine arbitrariness. It needs no divine intervention, to avenge in us violations of law. Sin, in its awfulness, has its revenge which never can be satisfied. "Every action," says Jean Paul Richter, "becomes more eternally an eternal mother than an eternal daughter." The soul disciplined in persistent wickedness, petrified in depravity, instinctively hides from God, and plunges wildly out into outer darkness, where she cannot hear the ineffably tender tones of his voice, or behold the glorious visions of her Creator. The sufferings of the lost, come moaning up from the depths of his own depraved and ruined nature. Omniscience cannot make a being happy who loves what God hates. Omnipotence cannot force blessedness into a soul that has lost its desire to be holy. If God cannot prevent the natural consequences of sin, his benevolence can in no way be impeached therefor. He cannot prevent sin destroying the nature in which it reigns triumphant. And the possibility of sinning is necessarily involved in freedom. Man has a capacity for decision, and decision is a necessity to him. But these are not penalties. Theologians have insisted that God inflicts positive suffering upon the finally impenitent. This is because the ultimate ground of immutable rightness had not yet been discovered. Any system of philosophy or theology that makes the ultimate ground of rightness either a sensibility or a subjectivity, or that makes the mere arbitrary will of God the foundation of a moral government, cannot fail to mislead as to the proper conception of the penalties of violated law. And the moment you conceive that the divine government rests upon the mere arbitrary will of an infinitely benevolent Being, you are logically coerced to pluck the final sting from all future suffering. You are forced by reason to open wide the doors of eternal hope to the incorrigible. But a clear apprehension of the ultimate reason of rightness dispels from the Bible and from theology all the positive inflictions of suffering upon the finally impenitent.

Moral government is the control of moral beings by rightful authority in the person of the ruler. But all moral government is pillared upon immutable rightness. Nothing, therefore, in moral government depends upon the mere arbitrary will of the infinite Executive. Benevolence, goodness, mercy can no more move God from rightness, on the one hand, than injustice, caprice, or favoritism could move him on the other. If God's benevolence could induce him to bless some persons unjustly, we could have no assurance that pure caprice might not incline him to blast others with an equal injustice.

The disobedience of moral agents puts to the test God's justice, firmness, authority and devotion to immutable rightness. The disobedient must not be permitted to disturb the peace and work and missions of the obedient millions. They must be prevented from ever permanently disturbing the blissful devotions and employments of celestial worlds. They must be held, where they will injure the moral universe the least possible. God is required by his absolute perfect rectitude to see that the disobedient are held in everlasting chains, and that the obedient are kept separate and sacred from their demoniacal presence and influence. If the Scriptures in such expressions as "Depart from me, ye that work iniquity," "Depart from me, ye cursed, into everlasting fire," seem to attribute infliction of penalties to the mere will of God, it is simply because immutable rightness imperiously requires it of him as the administrator of his moral universe. "The Scriptures," says Bishop Butler, "ascribe punishment to the divine justice which we know to be the natural consequences of wickedness." As immutable rightness and the consequences of its violation are independent of the will of God, the duty of its enforcement can never be optional with him. All that is positive in retribution is the execution of that which rightness inexorably requires. And all that rightness requires is that the incorrigible shall be held under restraint and kept from disturbing the devotees of holiness and obedience.

God's procedure in probation is to encourage virtue by benefits and discourage vice by sufferings. He does this to discipline men, if possible, out of wrong-doing. Under a remedial dispensation there is nothing incompatible in this. But this procedure never obtains in perdition. God does by way of earnest warnings announce to men the inevitable consequences of persistence in sin which await the disobedient in eternity. The wretchedness of the wicked is just as natural and just as inevitable as the happiness of the obedient. There is no mystery about either. The two classes cannot occupy the same place because their characters are different, their experiences are different, their affinities are different, and they can have no possible sympathy with each other. Those who have degraded themselves by persistent, willful sin must, in the nature of the case, be separated and kept separate from all the pure and holy in heart. God must make a separation between him that serveth him, and him that serveth him not. Accordingly our Lord says, Matt. xiii, 41, "The Son of man shall send forth his angels, and they shall gather out of his kingdom all things that offend, and them which do iniquity; and shall cast them into a furnace of fire: there shall be wailing and gnashing of teeth." Regarding the endless consequences of incorrigibility, as penalties inflicted by the arbitrary will of the ruler is the fallacy through which destroying angels are entering and paralyzing the Church of Christ. God cannot prevent perdition.

Many considerations render the doctrine of the future unhappiness of the wicked necessary for the consistency of the system of revealed truth. No other necessity can justify the incarnation of the Son of God, or put significance into the great atonement, or subjugate the depraved will to the divine will. The kingdom of heaven is never entered save through the violence inaugurated through a conviction of this awful truth of future and endless loss. Fear of perdition is really the incipiency of all holy lives. Belief in the unending consequences of sin is essential to persistency and earnestness on the part of the Church, in holy living and in evangelizing a ruined sin-cursed world. Nothing but this moving fear can perpetuate the militant church of Christ, antagonized as it is by the world, the flesh and the devil. Observation impressively and uniformly shows that those persons who embrace Universalism, annihilation, final restoration or æonism, without the influence of early indoctrination in contrary religious teachings are sadly wanting in zeal in saving souls from sin. And as to their own spirituality they are alarmingly indifferent. The remarkable apathy of those who advocate eternal hope as to the salvation of a ruined world urges upon us the great importance of a theology, that shall make plain and obvious the inevitable and endless consequences of incorrigibility. But the essential scripture doctrine of the endless separation of the incorrigible from the presence and favor of God is completely overthrown by the dogma of absolute prescience.

Though it is as certain as divine revelation can make it, that God does not, for reasons known only to himself, annihilate the fallen angels; and though one of the most earnest of the Universalists, John Foster, affirms that "the holy Scriptures are against Universalism," the Universalist affirms that an infinitely benevolent being could not create beings who he foreknew as a matter of fact would be eternally miserable. This argument has never yet been satisfactorily answered. I do not believe it ever can be answered, if absolute prescience be assumed. Universalism, with its variety of cognate errors, such as eternal hope, final restoration, æonism and annihilation of the wicked, will certainly obtain and increase in the world, paralyzing Christianity and ruining souls, just so long as absolute prescience is believed and maintained by the Church.

The first living woman in the Protestant Episcopal Church advocates the ultimate holiness and happiness of all mankind. The woman who exerts more influence on all the Christian Churches of this Nation than any other believes in final restoration. And the tetanic rigidity of Andover Calvinism has just elected to one of its theological chairs Dr. Newman Smyth, who, the "Cincinnati Gazette" says, "is not sure that the punishment of the wicked is to be unending," and who "approximates to the Roman Catholic doctrine of purgatory." Æonism holds that to affirm the ending of punishment is to fall short of Scripture, and to affirm its endlessness is to go beyond Scripture. I think it would be doing Dr. Smyth no injustice to classify him among this recent school of theologians. So long as he believes fore-ordination or foreknowledge, and traces logical links, eschewing absurdities, and keeps his intellect even tinged with the notion of mercy, he cannot escape this erroneous conclusion which is so de-energizing to the depraved will. You are authorized to censure Dr. Smyth's premises, but not his intellectual processes; they are inevitable if you admit the dogma of prescience. But upon this awful subject, how much wiser, more restraining and more energizing are the teachings of Dr. Orville Dewey, one of the serenest lights Unitarianism has ever produced, than are the hurried meditations of the gifted and excellent Canon Farrar. I read Dr. Dewey upon this subject many years ago, and his thoughts have exerted a most powerful influence upon my life and conversation. He says,

"The final suffering of a guilty mind wherever and whenever it comes must be great. This is the clearest of all truths, relative to the punishment of sin. Even experience teaches us this, and Scripture, with many words of awful warning, confirms the darkest admonitions of our experience. If sin is not repented of in this life, then its punishment must take place in a future world. Of all the unveiled horrors of a future state, nothing seems so terrific as the self-inflicted torture of a guilty conscience. It will be enough to fill the measure of his woe that the sinner shall be left to himself; that he shall be left to the natural consequences of his wickedness. There are no agents in the world to work out the misery of the soul like its own fell passions; not the darkness, the fire, the flood or the tempest. Nothing within the range of our conceptions can equal the dread silence of conscience, the calm desperation of remorse, the corroding of ungratified longings, the gnawing worm of envy, the bitter cup of disappointment and the blighting curse of hatred. The Scriptures were intended to leave on the mind the impression of some vast and tremendous calamity without informing us precisely what it is. They reveal our future danger, whatever it be, for the purpose of alarming us, and, therefore, to speculate on this subject in order to lessen our fear of sinning involves the greatest hazard and impiety.

"There is a high moral use of the awful revelation of the 'powers of the world to come.' It was intended and it is eminently fitted to awaken fear.

And, after all that has been said, I hesitate not to add, that we are in no danger of really believing too much. I maintain that every man should fear all that he can fear, and I actually hold a belief that affords the fullest scope for such feeling. It is not of so much consequence that any one should use fearful words on this subject, or violently contend for them, as that he himself should fear and tremble. What the retribution of a sinful soul is we do not know, but we know that such terms and phrases as 'the wrath to come,' 'the worm that dieth not,' 'the fire that is not quenched,' 'the blackness of darkness,' 'the fiery indignation,' 'the destruction of both soul and body in hell,' import what is fearful, and were intended to inspire a salutary dread. We know not what it is, but we have heard of one who lifted up his eyes, being in torment, saw the regions of the blessed afar off, and cried and said, 'Father Abraham, have mercy on me, for I am tormented in this flame.' We know not what it is, but we know that the finger of inspiration has pointed awfully to that world of calamity; we know that inspired prophets and apostles, when the interposing vail has been for a moment drawn before them, have shuddered with horror at the spectacle; we know that the Almighty himself has gathered and accumulated all the images of earthly distress and ruin, not to show us what is the retribution of a sinful soul, but to warn us of what it may be; that he has spread over this world the deep shadows of his displeasure, leaving nothing to be seen and every thing to be dreaded. And
10

thus has he taught us, what I would lay down as the moral of these observations and of all my reflections upon the subject, that it is not our wisdom to speculate, but that it is our wisdom to fear, for as I have said we are in no possible danger of believing too much relative to the awful theme and doctrine of future punishment." If fore-ordination and foreknowledge do not abandon their ground, Universalism will wave her scepter in triumph over all the ramparts of the republic of theologic thought. When that occurs the redemption of the race will be abandoned, and Jesus Christ will weep over his great failure to redeem a lost and fallen world. Christianity is a system of stern self-denial, self-sacrifice, and earnest life-long activities. No one will ever submit to this uncompromising system, engrossing all energies, who questions the existence of that utter outer darkness down into whose awful depths Jesus Christ so often, so solemnly and so feelingly pointed his warning hand.

If Christianity would survive as a life, as an aggressive force and as a transforming power in the earth, the Church must never cease declaring that the "wicked must be punished with everlasting destruction from the presence of the Lord and from the glory of his power." Let the ministry cease preaching eternal death, as the necessary consequences of incorrigibility, and its conversions, if any at all, will be superficial. They will be without deep and thorough regeneration of soul, and without reformation of life. The membership enrolled by such preaching will be inactive and worldly, and their piety will be easy and ineffectual. The doctrine of the eternal separation of the wicked underlies all the earnest piety and spirituality of the Church. Without it all is illogical in theology, and all is effeminacy in Christian zeal, endeavor and endurance. But absolute prescience, and endless sufferings of individual, souls are propositions perfectly and notoriously incompatible. The creation of immortal beings foreknown to be wicked, and interminably wretched can never be justified by any process of thought, either human or divine.

Dr. Minor Raymond says that this great perplexity may be escaped by supposing that "any condition of existence that infinite goodness will permit is better than non-existence," or by "modifying everlasting punishment to be something less than an endless consciousness of absolute unmixed wretchedness;" or by questioning " whether it were not better to affirm the total extinction of consciousness in the finally incorrigible than to deny the prescience of God?" But all of these subterfuges are wholly without even countenance, in divine revelation. We had better leave a stalwart difficulty than to overthrow divine revelation in our efforts to remove it. "Why God does not remove from the cradle to the grave one foreknown to be a desperado is a question," says Archbishop Whately, " which has never been answered by any religion, natural or revealed." If God can foresee pure contingencies with absolute certainty, he now sees that that innocent being will become a wicked outcast, pile regrets upon itself, break the hearts of all its friends, and then be forever miserable. If he allow it to remain, how can we defend, or proclaim, his infinite benevolence? God's moral character is infinitely dear to him, and hence he will not do, say, or teach any thing that would furnish a logical necessity for candid criticism upon his holiness. Were nescience of contingencies an imperfection, it would be infinitesimal to the imperfections prescience necessitates in the character of Jehovah. If we cling to prescience we must either surrender the moral character and goodness of Deity, or abandon the endless loss of the soul. If we abandon the teaching, that sin separates the soul eternally from its Creator in a state of conscious existence, Christianity cannot survive as a living reality for a century. And the human race will commit suicide, as it was ready to do on the advent of our Lord, in less than two hundred years after the annihilation of the Christian religion as a life and an aggressive power.

A theology that is fallacious in its fundamental assumptions, must inevitably lead to infidelity. Foreordination and foreknowledge render the irreversible eschatology of the Bible utterly indefensible and unbelievable. This fact overthrows prescience and demonstrates divine nescience of future contingencies to be a necessity alike to logic and to any admissible thought-system.

CHAPTER XIV.

DIVINE NESCIENCE OF FUTURE CONTINGENCIES IS NECESSARY TO THE HARMONIZING OF THE CALVINIAN AND ARMINIAN SCHOOLS OF THEOLOGY.

THE existence of these two opposing schools has been a great obstacle to the success of the Christian religion. It has occasioned needless discussions, diversions, detractions, distrusts and general loss of evangelical power. Arminianism, in substance, is as old as the Church of God. "Not one of the five points of Calvinism had any place in Christian thought, but to be opposed and reprobated, for the first four hundred years after the apostles," says Dr. Asa Mahan. And this assertion he strongly sustains by quotations of unquestioned authority. Calvin himself, with the divines of his school, all acknowledge that "the Christian Fathers, both of the Greek and the Latin Churches, all the way down to the age of Augustine, were wholly unmanageable for their purpose." "The whole Greek Church," says Dr. Schaff, "was synergistic." The peculiar tenets of Calvinism were the inventions of an era comparatively recent. They took their inception in the fourth century from Augustine. From his conversion until his forty-second year, Augustine himself entertained the Arminian views of the process of being saved. He says: "Sin is a volitionary evil. No one is compelled by his nature to sin. Whatever the cause of the will is, if it cannot be resisted, it is yielded to without sin. Man fell by his own free-will. God did not predestine his fall." He also declared that "the divine call was effectual only through the voluntary co-operation of the human will," and that "it is by our own free act of faith that we are cleansed from sin." But subsequently when Pelagius, who was an immovable Welshman, a pious monk, but not a preacher, sought about 350 A.D. to found a school of opinion, but not a sect in the Church, and assuming as his fundamental maxim, "What I ought, I can," and had affirmed that the human will of its unaided self was sufficient to initiate a holy life, Augustine hurriedly rushed to the opposite extreme, and declared that the entire work of human salvation was accomplished exclusively by the grace of God. Pelagius ignored the prevenient and ever attendant grace, as an indispensable factor in man's salvation, and Augustine ignored the other indispensable factor, the volitionary co-operation of the human choice and will, involving the powers of alternative choice. Then it was that Augustine definitely departed from the synergistic view, of this fundamental question in human salvation. He no longer regarded the divine call as an occasion of salvation, but declared it to be the efficient and exclusive cause thereof. This was the actual beginning of positive monergism in the Church of God. But this departure, which I regard as so prolific of evil, was not the only misfortune in the intellectual life of the great Augustine. However great our wonder at the intellect of Augustine, no man, unless he were inspired, however astonishing his powers and thorough his regeneration, could possibly escape all the evil and blinding effects upon his mental processes of advocating the system of manicheism, of believing for nine years in the existence of two eternal principles, one good and the other evil, and especially of living a life steeped in iniquity, until thirty years of age. Dr. Dorner says: "Great as is Augustine's merit, his system suffers under various and grave defects. He estimates human freedom too lightly, and leaves no place for free-will subsequent to the fall. With him faith is exclusively the work of God and that wrought in virtue of predestination. This doctrine, however, the Oriental Church never did accept."

It has been vehemently charged, that the Catholic Church founded its dogmas of its right to sell indulgences, and the virtuousness of falsehood in the interests of religion, and the right of the State to punish heretics, and even the establishment of the terrible Inquisition itself, upon the express teachings of St. Augustine. He taught, for instance, the remission of sins in baptismal regeneration, and the forgiveness of actual sins by "almsgiving, prayers and good works." Ecclesiastical history asserts that he, in common with many other Christian fathers, taught and practiced duplicity in the interests of religion, thinking, too, they did God service thereby. It also attests that in the long issue and bloody persecution of the Donatists, Augustine was the principal actor and instigator, controlling not only the whole of the African Church, but also the leading men of his country. He stood by, it is said, and exhorted hesitating officers to inflict upon the heretics, the penalties prescribed by legal enactments. Yet the Donatists were not heretical, on a single essential doctrine of faith. They believed that the unity and the freedom of the Church would be imperiled by its union with the State. "Their heresy," said Neander, "was a protest against confounding ecclesiastical with political elements. They made Catholicity to depend on purity, while Augustine made purity to depend on Catholicity." "No man can have Christ for his head who is not a member of his Church, and no separatist from the Church can be saved," replied Augustine. "But," says Dr. Wiggers, translated by Prof. Ralph Emerson, of Andover, "Augustine had the chief hand in the persecution of the Pelagians. That he was the most active in producing them is confirmed by all, both friends and foes." In reading the discussions of this great man, I cannot myself escape the conviction that he was sadly wanting in instinctive wisdom, intuitive insight, and moral sensibility, however wonderful may have been his other endowments; and, therefore, it does not seem to me that any special reverence is now due to the inventor of predestination, the inaugurator of monergism, and the founder of the Calvinian system of theology. For fifteen hundred years this system has been bold, aggressive, defiant, scholastic, dictatorial, fond of metaphysics, and marvelously successful among scholars and thinkers and holy men. For centuries Calvinians and Arminians, the two great armies of the Lord, have confronted one another, each vehement in the advocacy of its peculiar views. Both are partly right, and both are partly wrong. It is, therefore, one of the prime necessities of our holy religion, that they be harmonized in faith and combined in evangelical effort, as one glorious sacramental host for our risen Lord, marching distinctly but unitedly to the conquest of the world. And any devout essay toward such an object ought to be hailed by these opposing forces with acclaims of "Glory to God in the highest, and on earth peace and good-will to men." "For years," said Dr. Taylor, President of Wooster University, "I have been looking forward to a period of leisure, in which I might attempt what I regard as a great *desideratum*, the harmonizing of Arminianism with Calvinism." I think devout and discriminating Calvinians have often felt the pressing necessity of solving this great theological problem. But hitherto, all the herculean efforts that have been made have proved only abortive. A strong man, in the Princeton Essays, struggled hard at this mountain difficulty. The last irenicon that has fallen under my eye is in the "Homiletic Quarterly Review" for July, 1880. The writer, though an unflinching Calvinist, criticises Dr. Hodge severely. He charges him with suppression of evidence, passing in silence Scripture passages pertinent but opponent to his teachings, and of assuming, in the absence of facts, the existence of numerous texts in support of his own views. This writer denies that divine grace is irresistible, affirms that divine influences necessary to salvation are vouchsafed in good faith to all men, that the regenerate may fall away and finally be lost, and that the great atonement is universal. He thinks both Augustine and Calvin drew from what he regards manifest truth, incorrect inferences, and then regarded such inferences as a part of the truth. Thus this Calvinist surrenders three of the five points of Calvinism, in his effort to harmonize the two great systems.

An earnest Presbyterian, in the "Independent" for July, 1881, says, "The Congregationalists are to have a new creed, and I really wish *we* had a standard we could heartily believe for its truth as well as revere for its age. If we are to be the defenders of the faith we ought to have a faith which we can defend. It is an awful wrench upon the moral nature to attempt the defense of that which appears utterly unreasonable. It is so paralyzing to faith to have to apologize for the creed. It certainly would be in the interests of truth and of truthfulness to so amend our Confession of Faith as to relieve it of the parts which call for an apology."

But so long as we assume either universal foreordination or absolute foreknowledge, we pile up absurdities in theology, and contradictions in the word of God, higher than Mont Blanc, and we can no more argue them down, than we can speak that

THE FALSE PREMISES OF DECREES. 155

mountain into the sea. Arminians must abandon foreknowledge, and Calvinians must abandon fore-ordination. Divine nescience is necessary to the annihilation of the doctrine of election and reprobation. That doctrine rests on the false premises that the will of God is the foundation of right, that men are mere instruments in the divine hands, and that the human will is invariably determined by the strongest motive. These false premises are grave obstacles in the progress of Christianity. No one can question, that Calvinian Churches would have been vastly more useful in the past, and would be more powerful in the present, as an agency of evangelization, had they never advocated and defended the doctrine of election and reprobation. It does seem astounding, that fore-ordination should still require refutation. For while it satisfies nobody, it shocks almost every body. The Calvinist seldom tells just how he holds election and reprobation, and he will never allow an Arminian to state the case or formulate his proposition. The necessity of refuting predestination would not now exist, had Arminians manfully taught correct tenets on divine prescience. So long as they persist in maintaining absolute foreknowledge, fore-ordination will obtain among profound and logical thinkers. And just so long, will it shed its paralyzing influences, all along innumerable lines, through the Church of God. In this most impressive fact, I feel the deep necessity of the divine nescience of future contingencies. The forced approach of the modern moderate Calvinist toward Arminianism is not at all surprising, for Canon Moseley, himself a most rigid Calvinian, says: "Predestination belongs to a class of truths which do not admit of any statement. It cannot be stated without a contradiction of the divine justice and a contradiction of the free agency of man. To affirm that contingent events can be foreseen and can be the subject of previous arrangement and can come into a scheme of providence, is undoubtedly a self-contradiction."

But just so long as a belief in absolute prescience obtains, predestination will be bold, defiant, victorious and often intolerant. These two systems of theology, while they have been for centuries vehemently antagonizing each other, have really, in fact, most powerfully sustained each other. For one says the foundation of prescience is predestination; the other says the foundation of prescience, is the infallible futurition of all things. The Calvinian replies, If all futuritions are infallible, predestination, as I understand it, must be true, for all I claim is certainty, not necessity. Calvinism teaches that the human will is constrained, and it is a fact that the Bible is full of such teaching. But all passages referring to the constraint of the human will speak of man as a mere instrument in the hands of God. Arminianism teaches the freedom of the human will, with power of contrary choice, and the Bible is full of such teaching. But all the passages referring to the alternative liberty of the will regard man as an accountable being, free in all his choices. Whenever the human will is designedly constrained its action can be prevised; when it is left free, with power of alternative choice, its action is unforeseen and unforeknown, for nothing can be known in the absence of all evidence.

Accountability necessitates the origination of a choice between obedience and disobedience. The origination of a choice, precludes the possibility of its previous existence. For the origination of a choice, and its previous existence, are contradictories. If the choice have a previous existence, it cannot be an origination. If a free origination preclude previous existence, it may or it may not come to pass. If a free origination may or may not come to pass, it cannot be certain. If it cannot be certain, it cannot be foreknown. If God does not will an event, does not operate to bring it to pass, does not see it as the result of existing causes, then he can only know it, when the author of it, possessing the power of alternative choice, brings it from nonentity into existence. If the foreknowledge of an event which is not in the divine purpose, not in the divine desire, not a factor in his purposed government, not known by any mind in the universe, and which is infinitely deprecated by the Deity, and for which he is in no way or degree responsible, is not an absurdity then we have no use for the word absurdity.

Nescience of future contingencies is the new and great principle of exegesis, which redeems Bible theology from all the absurdities and contradictions which its advocates have crowded into it.

Believing a consolidation of the two great systems of theology to be a result to be devoutly desired, and possible of easy achievement, we will, in the spirit of candor and prayer, examine some of the recent utterances of the advocates of fore-ordination. My object now is to show how easily these statements can be, to say the least, fairly answered, and in this way, furnish satisfactory reasons for their immediate abandonment.* I am free to acknowledge, that these utterances cannot logically be replied to, by him who affirms absolute prescience. But, armed with the doctrine of divine nescience of future contingencies, I am not at all apprehensive of the result, even in the presence of the most gifted and revered of our Calvinians. For "thrice is he armed who hath his quarrel just." I by no means would enter these polemics *con amore*. I do it from a profound sense of duty I owe to the Church, so disturbed, unsettled and withered by unbelievable dogmas. Far be it from me to attack any branch of the "Church of God, which he purchased with his own blood." Victory, if that were possible in a game of wits, is a motive unworthy a man of common sense, much less of a Christian, who must account for the use of all his time, and meet in eternity all the influences he inaugurated in probation. But I see and feel the necessity of a union of all orthodox theologians, in order to contend against the aggressive and defiant powers of error and darkness, and to compass more

* For the full discussion of this subject see my work on "*The Foreknowledge of God and Cognate Themes.*"

speedily the conversion of the world to Jesus Christ. Theologians cannot differ fundamentally relative to the essentials of a true philosophy, the theology of the Bible, and systematic divinity, and all obtain a knowledge of the teachings of the divine word in their fullness, consistency and experimental power. In Calvinism, it seems to me, I see philosophical, theological and scriptural errors of great practical weakness and inefficiency. From its very inception down to this hour, it has been attended with suspense, hesitation and distressing questionings. "Calvinism," said Thomas Chalmers, "produces on some minds the most painful results." The teaching of the Friends "to await the moving of the Spirit," has chained the individual members, with all their capabilities of efficiency, in comparative inefficiency. But if it be clearly possible for us to reach a better comprehension of theological subjects, all who love our Lord and his Church should hear, examine, think, pray, and surrender whatever seems to be no longer tenable. I would, therefore, prayerfully attempt a harmony between Calvinism and Arminianism.

Universal consciousness attests to universal freedom, not, however, the freedom described by Jonathan Edwards, but the freedom that in its action is radically different from the action of constraint. "Though the will be bound by necessity," says Edwards, "still man is free if he is not constrained to act against that necessity, or is not restrained from activity in accordance with it." But our consciousness repudiates all coercion of the will by any influences, or by any unconscious constraining forces. Edwards confounded the power through which we act, with the susceptibility through which we feel. His logical skill was far in advance of his learning and general culture.

This shining proof of the incompatibility of liberty with constraint is strengthened by the absence of all consciousness of any constraint in our moral actions. The will involves two distinct powers, the elective and the conative. The elective power is selecting, preferring, deciding and choosing something out of the many. The elective involves the intellectual and the volitional. The intellect surveys the object, estimates its advantages or disadvantages, and the imagination clothes the same with charm or disgust as the case may be. After this deliberation the elective volition makes a choice. The conative power is purely volitional. Volition is the actual putting forth a resolve to attain that which the elective volition had chosen. A volition is not the result of an action, for it is action itself. It is not determined, for it is a determination. It is an act of the will, but not an effect on the will. Freedom is not a projecting from something back of itself. It is a true beginning, a veritable commencement, a real origination in the spirit, and not a constraining impulse from sense or from without. In this capacity of free origination there is a condition, or an arena for a proper libration between the happiness of a gratified want and the duty of a secured worth. Selfhood alone can create good or ill desert. In self-originating volition we locate the origin of character. No matter how subtle the influence that produces spontaneity, or that state in which the will acts consentingly under the law of constraint, whether it be *ab extra* or *ab intra*, it destroys all human accountability. No man can choose to go north unless at the same moment he can choose to go in some other direction, or in no direction at all. A current might bear him northward, and he might, consenting, yield to its pressure. But this could not achieve moral character. That personal worth can attach to an act in which and to which we are constrained by a superior power or influence, to the degree that renders impossible a different choice, is a manifest self-contradiction. It is, indeed, pronounced by all who do embrace it, and who believe that it does achieve moral worth, as something that is utterly inexplicable, so inexplicable as to be forever beyond the reach of reason. They regard it a mystery, which requires the broader light of eternity to make it appear rational. But if God controls men he never can punish them. For no power that controls can ever rightfully punish. "Unless man has the power to choose the good and to refuse the evil, he cannot be accountable for any action whatever," says Justin Martyr. Logic requires that in the kingdom of Providence, man should act consentingly under the law of cause and effect, that is, under the law of true constraint or restraint. Consciousness forces the Calvinian to believe in the freedom of his will. And the logical necessity for the constraint of the human will in the kingdom of divine Providence induces him to cover up or overlook the incompatibility existing between liberty and constraint under the ambiguous term of spontaneity, and then to claim his exclusive right to the phrase "self-determination of the will." But the will of man is never used as an instrument of Providence, in cases where moral character is involved. Its action involving morality belongs to the kingdom of free grace. In the kingdom of free grace, the will always acts willingly under the law of liberty, not consentingly under the law of constraint. God works all things in the kingdom of Providence according to the counsel of his own will, and hence he uses man as an instrument, but a consenting instrument. But in the kingdom of free grace he treats man not as an instrument, but as a free agent, and solemnly stands before his responsible creatures, and says to them, "Choose ye life or death." If in heaven God takes delight in a saint, he must respect him; but he cannot respect him any more than he can a flower, or a star, if all his choices to love and obey him were constrained by himself. Neither could he respect the angels, who cast their crowns at his feet did they do it by constraint. Binding constraint upon human liberty, where moral character is involved, is philosophically unthinkable. It is also a terrible reflection upon infinite benevolence, in that it does not equally restrain poor reprobates, with the chosen, favored elect. But we here also discover that it sweeps all mutual respect out of heaven, and robs God of all his enjoyment in the free determinations and devotion of creatures made in his own image and capable of creating a character worthy of divine respect. Notwithstanding these incontrovertible statements, the "Presbyterian Review" for April, 1880, says: "The power of alternate choice is indetermination, not self-determination. If a will is indifferent it has no determination of any kind, and can go with equal facility in any direction. But if it be actually in a state of self-motion or self-determination, it is committed and inclined to an ultimate end, and the facility of indifference and contrary choice is impossible." Webster and Worcester both define *indetermination* as "want of determination, a wavering state." *Indetermined* they define to be a state unfixed, unsettled. Indetermination is never suggestive of indifference, but it always implies deliberation, consideration of opposing reasons, or conflicting motives, in consequence of which the decision or the choice is deferred. But here this writer does not distinguish between the indifference of the will, and indifference of the person. Objects are either external or internal. The former is known by perception, the latter by consciousness. These objects impress the understanding and the sensibilities. The understanding appreciates and the sensibilities desire them. This appreciation and this desire are produced according to the law of cause and effect, and, being wholly passive in their nature, can have no causal efficiency over the will. If they had they would not be passive but active in their nature. The will would be constrained by them, and consequently characterless in its actions; and in that case the will could not create sin, and the incipiency of sin could only be traced to the Deity himself. If the human will is caused to act it cannot be accountable. But impressions on intelligence and sensibility are not activity, being is not doing. Our susceptibility of feeling is different from that power, by which we act or volitionate. When, therefore, objects, the attainment of which involves morality, impress the understanding and the sensibility, the whole person, save the will, deliberates. Between the impressions which objects make upon the sensibility and the understanding, and the action of the will, deliberation must necessarily intervene in responsible actions. When the objects presented to the understanding and the sensibility involve questions of obedience and disobedience, the whole person, save the will, is aroused and swayed to and fro. The battle rages between obedience and disobedience. All the capabilities of the person, the will only excepted, are summoned to the fray. The comparative desirableness and the comparative appreciation of the presented objects are contemplated. Memory, imagination, reason, intuition and conscience, all are active from within. Right, justice, duty, reverence, self-love, prudence, self-gratification, present realization, fear of ruin, hope of recovery from indulgences, all join in the solemn conflict. But amid it all the will sits serene because it is not an intellectuality, nor is it a passivity. It is not a receptivity, but it is a positive power of activity. Indeed, we have no more right to declare that the phenomena of the will are the same as the phenomena of feeling, than we have for saying that the phenomena of mind are the same as the phenomena of matter. At least, in this deliberation, the will sovereignly elects between the two objects, and then executively volitionates obedience or disobedience, and thus and thus only can character be created. This writer in the " Presbyterian Review" says: "If the will is indifferent it has no determination of any kind, and can go with equal facility in any direction." This is true, because the will is free, with a plurality of possibilities, before the person in whom that will resides. It is true because the will is the power of the person to act; and the way it does choose, at the end of the deliberation, fixes the quality of the act, and makes the character for the person. But in self-determination the *person* is not indifferent. He is attracted strongly in different directions. He is addressed by strong reasons, why he should determine in harmony with conscience, and he is assaulted by powerful temptations, to the gratification of desires in violation of law. Beneath the pressure of these opposing forces and influences, the person is not in a state of indifferency, but he vacillates to and fro between conscience and desire. This is demonstrated in the religious experience of any intelligent Christian.*

---

* While reading the proofs of this work, I was delighted to find in the " Princeton Review," for July, 1882, the following statements from Dr. George P. Fisher: "Choice is not the resultant of mo-

Though the will is a purely conative power, the person must realize the pressure of opposing attractions, competing reasons, or his will could not achieve character by electing and determining between them. Motives are objects or reasons addressed to our sensibilities. They are the essential conditions of choice, but it is impossible that they should control choice. It is impossible to do this for the reason that choice necessarily requires opposing motives, between which the will must make a responsible choice. This action of the will I prefer to call personic, for the reason that personality necessitates not only power over motives, but in addition power to elect between motives. A person must be sovereign over his sensibilities, sovereign over all motives addressed thereunto, or a consistent system of theology, and every thing

tives, as in a case of the composition of forces. Motives have an influence over us, but influence must not be confounded with causal efficiency. Motives are seen and felt, but a consciousness of pluripotential power ever remains in full vigor. We can initiate actions, by an efficiency which is neither irresistibly controlled by motives, nor determined by a proneness inherent in its nature. We can withstand temptations to wrong, by the exertion of an energy, which consciously emanates from ourselves, and which we know we could abstain from exerting. My consciousness attests that my acts are not the necessary consequences of antecedents, whether in the mind or out of the mind. The constraint of the will by exterior causes is fatalism. Spontaneity confined to a single path, by a force acting from within, is determinism. And both fatalism and determinism are promptly rejected by every unsophisticated mind. Indeed, the consciousness of self could never be evoked were the mind wholly passive under impressions from without. Self without freedom of will would be an inchoate being. Self-determination, as the very term signifies, is attended with an irresistible conviction that the direction of the will is self-imparted."

which involves morality, are whelmed in the vortices of confusion, perplexity and dismay. All that then could be left to the theologian, would be to shut his eyes and heroically affirm his dogmas, "uncaring consequences!"

But the vital point of virtue is the personic choice of goodness, and the personic rejection of badness. The essential point of vice is the personic choice of badness, and the personic rejection of goodness. This action is a simple indefinable idea, but it is the intuitive teaching of universal consciousness.

No one of us comprehends the union of an immortal spirit with a material body, but who hesitates heartily to believe it? No more ought we to question this personic action of the soul. "We have," says Archbishop Manning, "the same evidence of the existence of a self-determining power within ourselves, that we have of the existence of the material world outside of ourselves. This is an immediate and intuitive truth of absolute certainty." "Every man," says the distinguished Dr. W. B. Carpenter, "feels that he really possesses a self-determining power, which can arise above all the promptings of suggestion, and can mold external circumstances to its own requirements. And any system of philosophy which rejects the self-determining power of the will, or which regards the will as only another expression for the preponderance of motives, leads to the conclusion that man can be neither rewarded nor punished deservedly." Thus we see that the denial to man of the power of alternative choices, throws all theological thinking into spasms. It causes the philosopher to hesitate, whether he does know any thing with unquestioned certitude. But if philosophy and logic and the ever-pervasive necessities of thought systems, cannot demonstrate man's power of contrary choices, they can never establish any thing. The surrender of this great error in anthropology, namely, that man has not the power of contrary choices, is indispensable to any intelligent theology. The Calvinian must cease denying man the power of contrary choices, and the Arminian must cease confounding future contingencies with present certainties, or we must adjourn all hope of a harmonious theology. And until this is accomplished we cannot hope for interpretations of the holy Scriptures which will not be manifestly self-contradictory. Nor can we look forward to the combined effort of all orthodox Churches, in the evangelization of the world.

After finding so many and rare excellencies in Dr. Charles Hodge's "Theology," we were unprepared for the fallacies, psychological mistakes and lack of discrimination which he has incorporated in his chapter on the free agency of man. No wonder that one of his admirers recently declared that "much of his theology must be rewritten." Dr. Hodge states the issue fairly between the Calvinian and the Arminian, and inquires, "When a man decides to do a certain thing, is his will determined by the previous state of his mind, or can he with the same views and feelings decide one way at one time, and another way at another time?" To prove that the will is always determined by the previous state of the mind, he begins by assuming that this must be the case, or "the future choices of free beings could not now be certain." But his argument to prove that the future choices of free beings are now certain, is loaded down with a series of paralogisms, by which I mean unintentional fallacies. "God is free," he says, "but it is now certain that he will always do right." But God is not like a man, undergoing probation for the achievement of moral character and the attainment of endless rewards. Between the choices of the immutable Creator, and the determination of a limited creature, on probation for an eternal state of reward or retribution, there exists no point of analogy, that reaches the nerve of this argument. But even here the doctor takes for granted that for which he is without authority, namely, the present certainty of all God's future choices. God is certain, from everlasting to everlasting, to do right, but he may put forth millions of volitions which do not in any way involve questions of morality. This assumption of the present certainty of all God's future volitions arises out of limited views of the possibilities of the Deity, and logically, it would drag us out, perforce, into all the paralyzing mists and demoralizations of pantheism.

"There may have been," says Dr. Hodge, "a metaphysical possibility of evil in the choices of our Lord, still it was more certain that he would be without sin, than that the sun or moon should endure." But if there was a metaphysical possibility of evil in the choices of Christ, what ground has the doctor for declaring that all his choices were absolutely certain? But admitting this absolute certainty, between man and Jesus Christ there is no parallelism that touches the point in debate. The human consciousness of Christ, definite, positive and free as it evidently was, was, nevertheless, backed and barricaded by a consciousness made up of a union of the finite and the infinite, the human and the divine. This fact completely destroys all analogy between the two cases.

"Again," says Dr. Hodge, "the saints in heaven are free agents, and their future acts are now certain to be determined to the good forever." But the saints in heaven have successfully passed their probation; they are no longer on trial; they have achieved moral character, and are never again to be tempted or tested. Henceforth they will always choose in accordance with their achieved moral character. They are now established in holiness among the glorified, and they will certainly never choose to do evil. But what is there in this fact justifying the broad inference of the present certainty of all the future choices of those who, not only inheriting depraved tendencies, are enduring fierce temptations and undergoing fiery ordeals? But the truth is that moral beings, who see all things as they really are, never do choose evil. It is only when things are not seen as they really are, that free moral beings ever choose to violate God's law. Misapprehensions furnish the arena requisite for testing. His argument, therefore, from the impeccability of the saints in heaven, is also wholly unavailing for his purpose.

His next argument to prove that the future free choices of free beings are now certain, is, that "all who are born, will, during probation, certainly commit sin." But said the psalmist, "I was shapen in iniquity, and in sin did my mother conceive me." "By nature," says the apostle, "we are the children of wrath." And "that which is born of the flesh is flesh," are the words of our Lord himself. Our inward depravity renders it certain, though not necessary, that every child of Adam will, some time during its probation, violate God's law. But what ground is there in this fact for the inference that all the specific future choices of free beings are now certain in the divine mind? For this argument there is not and cannot be even the semblance of a basis. But it is very easy for any of us to find apparent arguments for a dogma, that we persistently cherish, as being necessary to our theological scheme. This whole argument of Dr. Hodge, to prove the present certainty of the future choices of free beings is entirely destitute of force and validity, and, therefore, it is of no possible avail in proving his main proposition, which is, that "the human will is always determined by the previous state of the mind."

The next argument of Dr. Hodge to prove that the will is determined by the previous state of the mind, is drawn from our consciousness. "We cannot conceive," he says, "that a man can be conscious that with his principles, feelings and inclinations being one way his will may be in another." How clearly does this statement betray the doctor's erroneous conception of human liberty.

He uses the phraseology that is appropriate to real liberty, while any liberty that can possibly involve accountability is foreign to all his thoughts. His only conception of liberty is a liberty to choose that, and that only, to which a man is unconsciously constrained. With such a pseudo view of liberty it would not be possible for him to conceive of the inclinations being one way and his choices being in another. Of course he could not conceive of water running up hill or of fire not charring flesh. According to his view the will is as truly under the same law of cause and effect, being controlled and coerced by predominant motives.

In physical forces, causes constrain effects, and if the same law obtains in the action of the human will, it would not be possible to conceive "that a man can be conscious that with his principles, feelings and inclinations being one way, his will may be in another way." But it is not difficult for any one who ascribes to man genuine liberty, the liberty or power of alternate choices, which is the only liberty that can possibly achieve rewardability, to conceive of him as feeling strongly inclined in one direction, and yet choosing in the opposite. He who cannot resist feelings swaying him in one direction and decide for the opposite direction, can be neither free nor accountable. Adam's soul was full of right views, correct principles, holy feelings and devout inclinations, and yet he put forth a sinful volition. And whoever has correct views of the human will can find no difficulty in conceiving of this simple fact of history. This personic action of the will is a simple, indefinable idea.

"All that consciousness teaches us upon this subject," says Dr. Hodge, " is that we could have acted differently, provided other feelings and views had been present in the mind." How difficult for the doctor, to arise from this conception of constraint, into the kingly splendors of moral liberty! But universal consciousness does testify that however strong may be the inclinations or the temptations to sin, the will can resist them all and decide in favor of virtue. There is in our deep convictions of accountability, and all that accountability implies, no proviso, as to the strength of our feelings and our inclinations and otherness of our views. We know that we are not things or instruments, but persons, and against winds and currents and attractions, we are masters of the situation. We know that we are moral sovereigns, and can resist, win and be heroes, or we can betray, lose and be traitors. If universal consciousness cannot be relied upon as to this point, it cannot be relied upon any where, as to our mental states. My own consciousness attests that however strong may have been temptations to sin, I could have resisted them all and done right. But for this terrible consciousness, every poisonous tooth of venom would be extracted. "But," says Sir William Hamilton, "freedom is a fact which is made known to us by our consciousness." Emanuel Kant also declares that "the liberty of the will is a matter of pure consciousness." Those acquainted with the writings of these profound psychologists, know that they use the term liberty to mean the power of alternative choices. The best authorities, as well as universal consciousness, therefore, pronounce the statement, and this argument of Dr. Hodge, to be absolutely fallacious. "It is inconceivable that man should be free," says the necessitarian. "This argument proves too little," says Sir William Hamilton, "for it is inconceivable that man should not be free, and consciousness is all on the side of freedom."

Dr. Hodge's next argument is, "that unless the will be determined by the previous state of the mind there can be no morality in our actions." But there can be no moral quality in actions if they are wholly determined for us, by the previous state of the mind. A free, original, independent, conscious choice between good and evil, is the *sine qua non* of every act that involves morality. The previous moral states of the nature, are the consequences of past free volitions, and to regard the consequences of past volitions as the sole causes of future volitions, excludes necessarily all moral qualities from future volitions. This would also annihilate from out of the soul its great endowment of liberty. Indeed, there would be no future use of a will, since the previous states of the soul control invariably the actions of the person. Unless I can sovereignly choose between competing motives, and can command *pro* and *con* feelings, to be submissive to the behests of my free-will, no act of mine can possibly possess a moral quality. If my will is coerced by any feelings, or views, or convictions, I can be neither a subject of praise nor dispraise. "If we are constrained," said Jerome, "there is no room for either damnation, or a crown."

Freedom of will when coerced by any thing pre-existing or existing, internal or external, no matter how subtle or latent, is simply an inconceivability. The idea that morality can attach to a volition, which is determined by the previous state of the mind, is a self-contradiction. Whenever the human mind embraces this contradiction, it is only to escape what it deems a greater inconceivability. I am free, only when I am not controlled to my determinations, by any reasons, feelings, convictions, inclinations, or even achieved moral character. I am free only when I determine my volition by an inherent, self-moving, personic power. I make the *nisus* myself or I forbear to make it, as I sovereignly choose, between conflicting motives. "If the will is constrained," said Origen, "man deserves no reward for virtue, and no punishment for vice."

Dr. Hodge says: "Man is responsible for his volitions, because they are determined by his principles and feelings, and he is responsible for his principles and feelings, because of their inherent nature as good or bad, and because they are his own and constitute his character." But how could feelings and principles be a man's own, unless he had freely chosen them, between contrary feelings, and then adopted them? The will sovereignly decides between virtue and vice, and then the principles and feelings follow, according to the law of cause and effect, the decision made by the will. I can obey God or not. If I disobey him my feelings necessarily become wicked. If I obey him my feelings necessarily become holy. And my feelings and principles can only become mine through my will electing obedience or disobedience to duty.

Dr. Hodge says: "Man is responsible for his principles and feelings because of their inherent nature." But whence did they receive that inherent moral nature? It was given them by some free-will. It is revolting to ascribe the inherent nature of evil principles and feelings to Deity. To do this Dr. Hodge hesitates and trembles; he therefore points down into the soul of man, intimating that possibly somehow or other, and in some inexplicable way, the morality of actions is to be sought for there. He positively affirms that the morality of actions is not to be sought for in the self-determining power of the will, because that power he vehemently denies. He says: "A man is free, so long as his activity is controlled by his reason and his feelings. The will is not independent, not indifferent, not self-determined, but it is always determined by the previous state of the mind. Man is free, but free agency is the power to decide according to character. Self-determination means that man is the efficient cause of his own act, and the reason and grounds of his determination are within himself." We thus see that

Dr. Hodge denies the self-determining power of the will, but affirms self-determination. If he would grant to self-determination the full power to choose between the attractions of sin and the claims of holiness, he would have a place on which to posit the morality of actions. But he vehemently denies the power of alternative choices, and therefore he has absolutely no place in which he can distinctly locate the moral quality of actions. It does, indeed, seem marvelous, that the good doctor could so ignore logic, psychology, common sense, and the pungency of the feeling of our accountability, in the interest of a system of faith, relative to the distinguishing features of which, we have in all its pulpits, the uniform eloquence of absolute silence. But the mystery is easy of explanation. We know that God did use men as instruments, and in so doing was compelled to put their wills under the law of constraint, and without the power of contrary choice, they chose consentingly as God desired. The Doctor's great defect was the limited view he took of the whole subject. Though as an instrument, man does choose just as he is constrained, as a free agent, he must choose for himself, and this necessitates the power of contrary choices. Regarding man as an instrument, in all kingdoms, he applied and followed his constraining principle, up into the dizzy heights of inexplicables and inconsistencies.

The Calvinian's view of spontaneity, is true in man's act, when he acts as an instrument. The error of the Calvinist is to carry this view of spontaneity up into the high realm of free agency. "But the character of the act," says he, "depends upon the motive, which determines the volition." True, the moral character of an act does depend upon the motive or intention, in view of which the voluntary being performs the act. Motive is a rational inducement to choice, and there must always be competitive motives, or choice is impossible. If the agent elects the sinful motive his act is sinful if he elects the holy motive his act is holy.

But this is an entirely different thought from the proposition, "that the motive determines the volition," that the motive controls the choice of the person in volitionating said actions. If the motive controls the will in its election and decision to volitionate the act, then the real origin of the act is in the objective motive, and not at all in the responsible man himself, not at all in the self-determining power of his will. That Dr. Hodge did not discriminate, between motive in the sense indicating the moral character of the act of a person, and motive in the sense of causing, coercing the act itself is truly surprising.

"If a man," says Dr. Hodge, "is independent of the previous state of his mind, his act has no moral character, for it does not reveal any thing in the mind." The object of a moral act is to obey and please Deity, and to gain moral excellence. It is not to reveal something already in the soul. If the object of the act is to reveal something in the mind, its motive is vain, useless, and leads to evil. The object of a moral act is merely to demonstrate the loyalty of a free will to the behests of the divine will. When Adam sinned he achieved sinfulness, but he did not reveal sinfulness, for there was no sinfulness in him to reveal. Adam's act was "independent of the previous state of his mind;" but had it no moral character? "A man's acts," says Dr. Hodge, "are not his if they do not express his moral character. Satan's revolt did not express his moral character, but was not his revolt, his to deplore?" "A volition is a revelation of what a man is," says the doctor. According to this, if a man's acts are wicked, then his moral nature must necessarily be wicked. Consequently before a soul can commit sin it must be full of sin. God, therefore, must have created an unholy nature in order to let sin into his universe. The doctor does not distinguish between achieving moral character, and manifesting it after it has been achieved. Julius Mueller says: "The state of the heart depends upon the primary decisions of the will. Character is formed by internal decisions. Moral character is of moral significance only so far as it has been produced by an act which is simply internal, that is the free inclination of the will. And he who regards a settled moral state as the original one for man, the *prius*, and that his every moral act and moral decision is its necessary outgo and effect, destroys altogether the idea of development."

Is it not sad to hear so distinguished a teacher in theology as Dr. Hodge confessedly is, say: "We confess we are free when we are self-determined, while at the same time we are conscious that the controlling states of the mind are not under the power of our will." Is it any thing less than amazing, to hear him declare: "The acts of men are necessary, but they are necessary in such a sense as to be, nevertheless, free, and necessary in such a sense as to be perfectly consistent with the moral responsibility of the agents." The acts of men are necessary, but necessary in such a sense as to be punishable! How a mind possessing such acumen could embrace a dogma so inexplicable, in itself so indefensible on the grounds of right, and so manifestly self-contradictory, is an enigma I am powerless to solve. Had there been truth in this statement Dr. Hodge certainly could have found it, and if he had found it, it would have been the happiest moment of his professional life to elucidate it before his admiring classes. The eminent psychologist, Dr. Reid, says: "If the determinations of the will be the necessary consequences of something in the previous state of the mind or of something in the external circumstances of the agent, then he is not free, and to affirm that when the state of the mind is the same the volitions will always be the same, is to reduce the human will to a mere machine, and to establish fatalism throughout the moral universe." Can any theologian afford to pass by this impartial testimony without prayerful consideration? "But," continues Dr. Hodge, "if the human will acts independently of the understanding and the feelings, its volitions are not the acts of a rational being. Man is a puppet or a maniac if his acts are not determined by his reason and his feelings. When a volition is contrary to the character, principles, inclinations, feelings and convictions of an agent it ceases to be the decision of an agent." It would seem that Dr. Hodge did not discriminate between the will as being determined and coerced by the feelings and the knowings, and the man as calmly electing between competing reasons and conflicting feelings, and then sovereignly determining what his volitions in the case shall be. Without competing reasons and feelings it is impossible for the will to elect and make a choice for which the person could be justly rewarded or punished. The moment the will is constrained, coerced by *any thing*, its freedom and accountability are annihilated. If this is not axiomatic, let us throw up the vocation of thought, and be humming-birds till the sunset of life. "If I have not the power to resist God's will I have not the power to submit to God's will," is the exclamation of the distinguished Dr. Dorner. "The will," says Dr. Hodge, "is not independent, not indifferent, not self-determined, but it is always determined by the previous state of the mind. Man is free just so long as his volitions are the conscious expressions of his mind. He is free, but his will is not free in the sense of being independent of reason, feeling and consciousness. An act performed without reason, without object, and for which no reason can be assigned, is as irrational as the act of a brute." But the power of contrary choice does not imply that the will is independent of reasons, feelings and consciousness, or that man acts without reason or objects or intentions.

Reasons, objects, intentions are essential to moral action, and there must be not only reasons for volition, but also competing reasons for contrary and opposite volitions to afford the free agent an opportunity to elect between them. In this modified sense the volitions are not independent of reasons and feelings. But the will is absolutely independent of the reasons and feelings in the sense that they may determine its volitions. And that it should be otherwise is utterly inconceivable. The will is not independent of occasions of acting, but it is independent of coercing causes or constraining influences. Is it possible Dr. H. could not discriminate this distinction? Because the will must be self-poised between conflicting motives, Dr. Hodge affirms that the will is "indifferent." Calvinian metaphysics seem to me to be incapable of distinguishing between the person and his will. But there is no more difficulty of distinguishing between the person and his will than there is of distinguishing between the person and his sensibility, or between the person and his cognitive faculty. The last two distinctions are no more important than the first; but Calvinians delight in calling the will the person. Now the will may and must be indifferent, but the person is not indifferent. The person is tested powerfully in opposite directions whenever he is called upon to decide moral questions. How entirely the good doctor fails to distinguish between testing influences brought to bear upon the person, of opposing motives, which are necessary to the achievement of character, and the control of those motives over the volitions of the human will! It certainly would be mockery in Deity to endow us with self-hood, and then deny us an arena on which to assert that self-hood, or an opportunity to achieve self-respect for ourselves, or a possibility to establish our rightful claim to divine rewards.

The next argument is, "If the will is not determined by the previous state of mind, then there must be an effect without a sufficient cause. The efficiency of the agent is a reason for the existence of the volition, but it is not a sufficient reason for the volition being as it is rather than otherwise." But I reply, Efficiency is not the only quality or faculty of a person. In addition to efficiency it is essential to a person that he possess the power of alternate choices between competing influences. Man as an instrument can be led to choose consentingly under the unconscious constraint of forces brought to bear upon him. But in this view he cannot be a person. A hurricane has efficiency, but it is destitute of personality. Efficiency in a being without the power of alternate choices is incapable of personal actions or efforts. The true definition of a person is a being capable of sovereignly deciding between competing influences, wise or unwise, holy or unholy. A person can be coerced in accountable acts neither by reason nor by feeling nor by Deity himself.

The free-will is a cause, not an effect, and it

requires nothing outside of itself to account for its acts. The sufficient reason, therefore, why the agent exerts his efficiency in one way rather than in another is the splendid fact that he is a person and not a thing. He moves, he is not moved. The person is the cause and the volition is the effect. Hence the self-determining power of the will does not at all involve an effect without an amply sufficient cause. How the doctor could have made this statement with any proper conception of personality is a great mystery. My choice of obedience to Jesus is the effect of my sovereign free-will. Freedom is the essence of personality, and consciousness is the feeling of personality. Self-motion is the distinctive attribute of spiritual agents. In and of itself a spirit can act in either of divers ways. Material causes can act but in a single way and with but a single result. A spirit is a person, and personality implies self-consciousness and self-determination. A spirit therefore cannot be confined to a single way of acting. The self-motion of a spirit therefore cannot be an effect without a cause. Indeed, all causes originate in free-wills. Philosophy will not allow us to locate causes anywhere but in mind. The causes that control in material things receive all their efficiency from the volition of a spiritual being, who could have willed material forces to act according to different laws. Is it not then surprising that Dr. Hodge should clog, chain, and degrade a spirit with the same kind of causation that controls in material forces, when that kind of causation originated in a self-moving spirit, and receives all its efficiency from that spirit? Because the will is not controlled by motives, nor by the previous state of the heart, nor by subtle influences, he has no warrant at all for inferring that its act is an effect without a cause. It is an effect of the highest conceivable cause, a self-moving spirit possessing the power of contrary choice. Assume that spirit causation and matter causation are identical in kind, and fatalism holds us in her Gorgon grasp, turning us rapidly into stone, and the awful system of necessity comes down upon us as black night upon a troubled ocean. Assume the universal reign of that kind of causation that is regnant in material things, and every thing that is worthy of thought is lost forever, and God himself is frozen into everlasting inactivity, indifference, and inability. But again the doctor says: "If the will acts independently of the previous state of the mind then our volitions are isolated atoms springing up from the abyss of the capricious self-determinations of the will." But I ask, where else did sin come from? Sin exists and must have had an origin. Either it came out of that capricious, uncertain abyss, or it emanated from God. There is no middle ground: sin originated in a creature free-will or the divine free-will. Sin without the action of some free-will involves contradiction. It is simply an exercise of a free-will in opposition to the right. The declaration that sin came from out the divine free-will is the blackest of all blasphemies, for God's moral character is infinitely dear to him.

Dr. Hodge denies that sin came out of that capricious abyss of the self-determination of the will. He says, (page 537,) "The reason why any event ever comes to pass is that God so decreed it." No wonder he exclaims with evident hesitation and tremor, "It may be difficult to reconcile the existence of innate evil dispositions in the soul of man, with the justness and goodness of God. It is, indeed, repugnant to our moral judgment that God should create a malignant being, but this has nothing to do with the question whether moral dispositions do not owe their character to their nature." But why should the good man cling to a system of theology that necessitates such heart-disturbing meditations? Neither psychology, nor logic, nor common sense, nor Scripture, nor the success of Christianity, nor the comforts of the Gospel, require of him any thing of the kind. Ten thousand times better repudiate such an origin of sin, and then trace its incipiency down into that uncertain abyss of the self-determining power of a free-will, rather than therewith to darken the throne of the Eternal, and fasten an appalling dubiety on the moral character of Jehovah. And yet John Calvin made the divine will the originative cause of evil. "All the descendants of Adam," says he, "fell by the *divine will* into that miserable condition in which they now are." No wonder that that distinguished Presbyterian, Dr. Duryea, a man so eminent for his union of analytic and synthetic ability, recently in a public manner positively denied that he was any longer a Calvinist.

But, without any controversy, the new Arminianism sends a line of living light through this whole subject. It leaves no point unilluminated, and piles up no vexatious contradictions in its path.

But the doctor continues: "On the hypothesis that the will determines itself there can be no such thing as character." Here he does not discriminate between a created nature pure and spotless as it came from the hands of the Creator, and an achieved character. Character necessarily involves the ethical. Moral character refers to volitionating, moral goodness refers to the nature resulting from moral character. The nature of a being may be perfect, but he can have no moral character until he volitionates in view of a moral standard placed before him. The natures of fallen angels were without sinful tendencies, but they had no moral character until they volitionated in view of divine commandments. Adam was created without the slightest bias to evil, but he had no moral character until he volitionated between obedience and disobedience. Religion is acting in view of pleasing the Deity. Morality is acting in view of pleasing immutable rightness. Virtue is volitionating concordantly with morality. Vice is volitionating discordantly with morality. Moral character is the result of virtue on the nature of the spirit. Piety is the result of religion on the nature of the spirit. Holiness is a state of freedom from sinful affinities. If the inward nature determines the will, how could moral evil ever have transpired? If the moral state determines the will, God must have created Adam with a bad moral state, for he did volitionate wickedly. He actually achieved a bad moral character. This character was either created by himself or by his Creator. As the latter supposition is awfully blasphemous, we are coerced to the conclusion that Adam, though possessed of a pure nature, created for himself a sinful character. The only possible creator of character is the free-will of an accountable being. Neither a pure sinless nature, nor an achieved moral character, can determine the will. Holy beings have volitionated sinfully and achieved wicked characters, and beings with wicked characters often volitionate obediently to God. If character coerces volition, the good man can achieve no rewardability in good volitions, and the wicked man can achieve no punishability in wicked volitions. So if the will is determined by the previous state of the mind, character is an inconceivability. A spirit is able to produce something different from itself, or theology is inconstructable. Reader, is not the proposition of Dr. Hodge, that "if the will determines itself there can be no such thing as character," utterly defenseless? Good men do put forth wicked volitions, and bad men do put forth good volitions; and what a free-will, acting under the law of liberty, will do, no one can ever know with absolute certainty. While maintaining that spontaneity does not constitute free agency, Dr. Hodge charges inconsistency upon Jonathan Edwards for embracing in his signification of the term *will*, "all preferring, choosing, and being pleased with, or displeased with," and then advocating a theory which is applicable to the will only in the sense of being the power of self-determining. But Dr. Hodge himself says, and his system forces him to say: "The word will indicates all the desires, affections, and even the emotions. It has this comprehensive sense when all the faculties of the soul are said to be included under the two categories of understanding and will." But although this twofold division of the mental powers once was prevalent it was long since repudiated. Noah Porter says: "The threefold division of the powers of the conscious ego, intellect, sensibility and will, is now universally adopted by those who accept any division of the faculties. It has taken the place of the twofold division which formerly prevailed, into the understanding and the will, according to which, the sensibility, or the soul's capacity for emotion, was included under the will; and the affections, as they were usually called, were regarded as phenomena of the will." "Dr. Reid," said Porter, "limits the will to the capacity to determine or to choose, excluding from it the capacity for both emotion and desire." Dugald Stewart adopted the same division. How, then, Dr. Hodge could be uninformed of this fundamental and universally admitted fact in modern psychology is to me an inexplicable mystery.

He defines motives to be "those inward convictions, feelings, inclinations and principles which are in the mind, and which impel or influence the man to decide one way rather than another. These motives are the reasons which determine the agent to assert his efficiency in one way rather than in another. They are causes, in so far that they determine the effect to be thus."

"The will is never self-determined; it is always determined by the previous state of the mind." But, I ask, cannot our natural dispositions be controlled through the ability which belongs to the will? Cannot the will, through universal prevenient grace, prevent the development of these natural dispositions of the soul?

"Man is free so long as he is controlled by his reason and his feelings." Of course a rational agent must always consider the reasons and his feelings in any responsible act. But if he is compelled to choose to act under the influence of one set of reasons and feelings rather than another set of reasons and feelings, he is not a rational agent, but he is a thing, and incapable of accountability. "If," as Dr. Hodge says, "the will is determined by the feelings, principles, character and dispositions which at the moment constitute a man a particular individual," where can we locate accountability? His own deep, significant silence answers, Nowhere. Could he read his inner consciousness, I think he would see a reference to the eternal decree of the universal Sovereign.

"I deny," says Dr. Hodge, "the self-determining power of the will; I do it because it is a denial that the will is controlled by motives. The power of contrary choice means that with the same state of mind and feeling the choice might have been different. The will always decides in favor of that which promises to be desirable. It is always determined in favor of that which under some aspect or for some reason is regarded as good." We cannot but regard these statements as an effort to dignify mere constraint of the will by the respectable nomenclature which belongs to the power of alternative choices. "If a man," says Dr. Hodge, "may act in despite of, and contrary to, all influences which can be exerted upon him, then it must remain forever uncertain how he will act."

But this "uncertainty" presents no difficulties, for impossibilities limit omniscience, as well as omnipotence. Future free acts are not subjects of present knowledge. Not to know them, therefore, is not the least limitation upon the perfection of omniscience. Omniscience, even, cannot see evidence where no possible evidence exists. My forging a note on the morrow is a thing no more impossible than the disobedience of Eve. If there is any evidence that on the morrow I will forge a note, who can tell where that evidence exists? It is now farthest from my thoughts, and in myself I see no evidence of the specified perfidy. If no evidence of it exists in my own mind, it can exist in the mind of no other created being. God has no evidence of it in his decree, for he never decreed it. He has no evidence of it in his desires, for he trembles at the thought of it.* But you say God foresees the influences that will be brought to bear upon

---

* Dr. Dorner says: "The knowledge of free acts cannot reach God by his self-intuition. Free causalities would not exist if by mere self-intuition God knew their realization."—Vol. i, p. 326.

me leading me to choose the wicked deed. But, if God foresees influences acting upon my will, to that degree of its control, he can only trace those influences on the line, and according to the law, of cause and effect. But if the causal incipiency of my act of forging lies in the objective motive, then I am shut up to a single result, namely, the crime of forging. The law of cause and effect is limited always to a single result. But if I am shut up to a single result, I am constrained in my action. But the law according to which accountable acts are performed cannot be the law of objective constraint. Acts performed according to the law of constraint cannot achieve moral character. Responsible acts must be performed according to some law totally different. They cannot, therefore, possibly be foreseen in tracing influences along the lines of cause and effect. But, the tracing the influences of motives, in accordance with which I shall certainly choose to forge a note, in order to find present evidence that I will, assumes that the previous state of the heart and mind invariably determines the choice of the will. In desire there is a susceptibility that longs for gratification, but no efficiency. It is unthinkable to attribute to a sensibility a causal efficiency. We feel with our feelings, but act with our will. But this assumption that the previous state of the heart determines the choices I have shown to be an inexcusable fallacy. But, admitting that God now sees evidence of my future forgery in the influences that will be brought to bear upon me, where is his infinite mercy that he does not in the fatal moment strengthen me correspondently for the combat, or spirit me away from the scene of the conflict? But the whole theory contradicts the Scripture, which says: "He will not suffer you to be tempted above that ye are able; but will with the temptation also make a way to escape, that ye may be able to bear it." We are thus driven, as the final resort, in search after present evidence of my future forgery, to the subjective action of my own freedom of will, the only place where character or accountability can possibly be located.

After writing the above I was astonished to find upon a single page of a recent edition of Dr. Hickok's Philosophy a cluster of fallacies upon this subject. One objection to the liberty of the will which has been urged is that it precludes the possibility of its future determinations being now foreknown. Nothing that now exists can determine that an avoidable event will not be avoided. That event has no necessary connection with any thing that now exists in nature.. Dr. Hickok replies that "this avoidable event cannot be foreknown through any successive changes in nature, but a spirit which might know all the inner and outer occasions in which the agent shall be, might find ground of certainty in these very facts." But, if it be impossible to foreknow through any successive changes, so far as we are now able to trace them, the inference ought to be that the same impossibility of foreknowing would be true in tracing the changes that now lie beyond our vision. The doctor's inference, therefore, that a spirit might foreknow, is wholly without foundations. How does he know that a spirit *might* foreknow through the occasions of the choice of a free spirit? Of this he has no evidence at all. But his reply, to carry any force to the objector of human freedom, ought to be, a spirit *can* thus foreknow. But this would be a manifest begging of the whole question in debate. The doctor inquires, "Must God foreknow only as he can look through the necessary sequences in nature?" This implies that the doctor had a conception of some other mode through which God could foreknow a future contingent event. But of this mode he gives us no intimation, but at once returns to the old mode and says: "God foreknows the event by tracing the connection between the event and the inner and outer occasions in which the free agent shall be." But this is the old fallacy of Dr. Samuel Clarke, of seeking in the objective occasions of choice, the certainty of that choice. This he cannot do without locating causality in " those inner and outer occasions of choice." But this cannot be done without destroying freedom and sweeping accountability out of the realms of thought. A free, self-originated self-determination cannot possibly in fact, nor conceivably in theory, possess any causal anterior, back of the pure action of the will. Creation implies origination into existence of that which did not exist in any of its constituents. This action I would prefer to call personic or godlike.*

* Dorner creates the word "solity" to express aloneness.

God's will is free absolutely; it is controlled by no objectivities, biased by no impulses, and can never be determined by motives. Before God created any thing there were no objectivities to influence him, and, being perfect in his sensibilities, his will sat serene, indifferent, perfect, unbiassed by any impulses. He was ready to act or not to act —to act in any one of divers ways as rational or sensitive occasions might arise in his own infinite thoughts and sensibilities. Without intellect he could not know, without intellect and sensibility he could not feel, and without a faculty as distinct and different from intellect and sensibility as sensibility is distinct and different from intellect he could not act. Being free, volitional, sovereign, originative and creative, his will acts in its own limitless self-determination and fathomless self-hood. If this be not so, then God, too, is bound in the chains of necessity, and theological blackness of darkness presses heavily upon us all. In this manifest psychology of the divine volitions we read the true psychology of human volitions; for man was created in the image and likeness of God. If the human will does not act like the divine will, he is not in the image of God, and the grandest feature of the Deity is absolutely without any representative upon the earth. And if the process of human volition differs from the process of divine volition, then we never could have known or dreamed that God's volition is free, sovereign, originative and accountable. Human volition, I therefore pronounce to be godlike in its capacity and godlike in its action. Beyond this ultimate truth we need not seek and ought never to inquire. But the declaration that God's present evidence of my future forgery lies in the influences he foresees will be brought to bear upon me, is simply a begging of the whole question in this profound debate. Calvinians freely admit this constrained action, and are imperious in its affirmation. Arminians are inconsistent and illogical enough to ascribe to the human will the power of contrary choices, and yet to assume, in absolute prescience, a premise that necessarily shuts up the will to a single result. In this way they pusillanimously chain themselves to the Calvinian car, and meekly follow in its somber and saddened train. We, therefore, confidently affirm that there is now no possible evidence in any mind, created or uncreated, that on the morrow I will consent to the crime of forgery. Not, therefore, to foreknow it could be no limitation upon the omniscience of Deity.

But how misleading and confusing all the plausible declarations of Dr. Hodge relative to human freedom and accountability, when in explaining why one man repents and another does not, he expressly declares that "God gives a holy influence to one man that he does not give to another." This holy influence, sovereignly given, the chosen one, the elect one, "must yield to and follow." This means that eternal life is fore-ordained to some and eternal death to others of the race. It means election, reprobation, a limited atonement, irresistible grace and final perseverance. It means predestination; and predestination, says Calvin, "is the eternal decree of God, by which he hath determined in himself what he would have become of every individual of mankind. The gate of life is closed to them whom he devotes to condemnation. He reprobates for no other cause than his determination, for no other cause than because he wills it. And to inquire into the cause of the divine will is exceedingly presumptuous, for it is the cause of all things that exist." This teaching of Dr. Hodge makes man the passive instrument of a secret power. The effectual motives that determine him impinge upon his will at a point outside of his perception and cognition. But no system of a will conditioned in its antecedent grounds of preference has ever satisfied the common conviction. "The will is a free deliberate tendency to act, while desire is a blind fatalic tendency to act," says Sir William Hamilton. "It is not motive that makes the man, but it is man that makes the motive," says Coleridge. "The will," says Dr. M'Cosh, "is self-determined; mind is a self-acting substance, and, therefore, it is independent. The determining cause of any volition is not an anterior incitement, but it is the very soul itself, by its inherent power of will. Man is just as free as God is free. Morally man is as independent of external control as God ever must be." Man's freedom is his power of being and doing otherwise, exclusive of outward forces or inward cravings. Alternative action requires that there be a conflict between a susceptibility of sensibility, and a susceptibility of rationality. This capacity for alternative action is in the supernatural only. God is supernatural, angels are supernatural, and the human soul is supernatural. It is supernatural because it can resist, control and conquer nature, which is the empire of mechanical necessity. If the will is not above nature there is no supernatural in the universe. If creation is not the result of a volition there can be no personal Deity. "In my will I am conscious of supernatural agency," says L. P. Hickok. "Will is that which originates an act," says Coleridge. Will is an operating cause, a determining principle. "It is causality, efficiency from which all action springs," says Julius Mueller. "The mother of all error," said the judicious Hooker, "is the mixture by speech of things which by nature are divided." Who then can defend Dr. Hodge from the charge " of darkening counsel with words without knowledge?" My destiny is to make my will God's will, but lest I possess myself I cannot surrender myself. If extraneous influence control me, God is responsible for my destiny.

I have given this protracted examination to the metaphysics of Calvinism, as taught by Dr. Hodge, because he is the latest and the most authoritative expounder thereof, and because he is the acknowledged Corypheus, the reigning king in Calvinian theology. A recent writer says: "Hodge's theology in Princeton is reverenced next to the Bible." And now can any one who loves Christianity more than he loves Calvinism, fail to see that these teachings of the great defender fasten no valuable convictions on the minds of his intelligent readers? Can any one avoid seeing that he does not relieve Calvinism of any one of its painful mysteries, or soften a single one of its stern presentations. They must see that he administers no relief to oppressed hearts, affords no inspiration or fortitude to probationers in the fierce battles of life.

To silently cherish the tremendous error of election and reprobation, weakens confidence in logical processes, disturbs the peace, and lessens the progress of the soul in knowledge of divine things. But persistently to advocate it and defend it, greatly embarrasses the mind of its advocate, and also the great work of saving a lost world. In the sacred name of Him who died upon the cross for us all, let it now be abandoned, and abandoned, too, with a shout of devout relief and thanksgiving. This entreaty to theologians, and this prayer to Deity, find, I doubt not, warmest responses in the noble hearts of not a few Calvinians. If a system of religious teaching is antilogical, antipsychological, anti-scriptural, and antagonistic to human instincts and intuitions, what can justify its continuous maintenance? For the continued existence and proclamation of the dogma of eternal election and reprobation, I cannot conceive of a solitary plausible excuse. For "virtue," said Basil, "must certainly come from the will itself, and not from its constraint."

No seeker after divine truth can read without distressing confusion the following statements found in a recent number of the "Baptist Quarterly Review," from the pen of the Rev. Dr. Augustus H.

Strong, President of the Baptist Theological Seminary, located at Rochester, N. Y. I have conscientiously arranged some of his contradictory affirmations, one over against the other, and to some of them have subjoined brief replies.

The argument in these articles of Dr. Strong being so similar to that found in Dr. Hodge's chapter on Free Agency, any additional reply from me might seem unneeded. But as Dr. Strong justly stands so grandly before the Baptists of America as a scholar, thinker, theologian, and minister of our holy religion, it might be well to call the reader's attention to his most matured views, as another index, showing how the dogma of election and reprobation is intrenched in all our Calvinistic schools, councils, theological seminaries and fountains of thought and opinion. As I have had to attempt to scale so many strongholds of error with the same ladder, should I at any point be open to the charge of repetition, I trust to find an excuse in the generosity of the reader. My object is, at all hazards of criticism, to get my thoughts clearly before his understanding.

Dr. Strong says: "Consciousness testifies to human freedom, but this consciousness of freedom in volitions we must set down side by side with another consciousness, the consciousness of a malign will beneath, that hinders persistent choice of the right and binds us to a deeper necessity of will. For the will may be free while volitions are determined by the inward character. The only freedom I know is the manifestation of character, and the character makes the motives. The cause of an act is made up of two parts, the power that did it and the reasons for which it was done. The first is the efficient cause and the second is the occasional cause. The causes of all volitions lie wholly within the mind, and the strongest motive rules the preference. All motives originate in the underlying regions of the desires. The desires and longings of the soul are states of the will. The whole stream of moral tendency is in the realm of the voluntary, and belongs to the will. The will is the principle of mental movement, the whole impulsive power of man's being, the whole tendency and determination of the soul to an ultimate end, and the settled appetencies in which the person puts forth power. The will may be free while the direction and form of the volitions are determined by the character. Defining will as the faculty of volition regards only its most superficial aspects. As a faculty of volition the will is an efficient cause, a *causa causans*. But the will in this narrow sense is under the law of the will in its larger and deeper sense, and the will in its larger and deeper sense is a *causa causata*. In this deeper sense the will embraces the whole stream of our dispositions, desires and moral tendencies."

"Man is a cause, and he is also caused. He determines, but he also finds himself determined. He acts freely, but the direction of his acts is furnished by a voluntary nature that reaches down beneath his consciousness. He cannot sunder the faculty of volition from the directing powers beneath. He possesses a formal freedom, but he is in real slavery. He is a swimmer in the stream, but the current is too strong."

"The formal freedom of the will, considered as the faculty of volition, may still subsist, while yet the will, considered as the underlying movement and current, is in bondage. The fact that I have power to will explains the fact of my willing, but it does not explain the fact of my willing this rather than that; I am only free to do what I desire to do. Freedom never shows itself except in the choice of what we like. What dignity or value is there in a wild contingence which may unintelligently will to its own ruin? To maintain that indeterminateness is essential to liberty is to contradict all experience and all consciousness."

"The power to decide against one's character and against all the motives operating on the mind at the time is a power which not only has no existence, but of which we have no power to conceive. And when I am told that the secret of a pure consistent life or of a bad life is simply a choice I feel that it is an impertinence."

"Such a theory of the will wrecks itself on the solid rock of our primitive convictions, that every effect must have an adequate cause. We could not in the past have chosen differently from that which we actually did choose. A correct and consistent view of the will is indispensable to present the Gospel in its completeness and power."

After reading these contradictory utterances I was not only amazed, but greatly grieved. Dr. Strong ignores the universally accepted division of psychological activities into intellect, sensibilities, and the will. He clings to the bottom assumption of the infidel Hobbes and the Christian Edwards.

Fallacies pervade the works of Jonathan Edwards, from his failure to distinguish the will from the affections. "The difference," says he, "between natural necessity and moral necessity lies not so much in the nature of the connection between the two terms, as it does in the nature of the two terms themselves." The connection, then, according to Edwards, in natural necessity and moral necessity, is the necessary connection of cause and effect. The skeptical Buckle, in his History of Civilization, assumes that the human will acts uniformly under the law of cause and effect. To the infidel this is, perhaps, a necessity; but for a leading divine, at the head of a school of Christian prophets, to classify the will under the sensibilities must be discouraging to every thoughtful and intelligent inquirer after the truth on which his eternal salvation depends.

Dr. Strong, in his meditations, does not discriminate the all-important psychological fact that it is impossible for a free being to choose a thing unless he can at the same moment refuse to choose that thing. He overlooks the necessity that back of all moral actions lie competing motives for and adverse to every responsible volition. These opposing motives always impress the sensibilities, but never constrain free choice. They are the required conditions of responsible action, and they are indispensable to moral accountability because they afford the needed opportunity of making choices. "To a choice a plurality of possibilities is essential," says Julius Mueller. Unless I am an originator of responsible choices between opposing attractions and competing preferences I can be neither a subject of praise nor of dispraise. "Neither rewards nor punishments are just," said Clement of Alexandria, "if the soul has not the power of choosing or abstaining."

The reason of any act is the motive in view of which the will, which is the cause of the act, ultimately acts. The will not only requires occasions for its action, but it requires alternate occasions. A physical cause can produce but a single effect. Gravitation cannot say, I will attract, or I will not attract. Fire cannot say, I will char flesh, or I will not char it. But a person can say, I will obey, or I will not obey. The human will can produce any one of many effects. A unipotent effect requires a unipotent cause. But an alternate effect requires an alternative cause. A complete cause produces its effects uncausedly. Such a complete alternative cause is the will of man.

A material cause produces phenomena identical and in constant repetition, but the will can produce phenomena variant and in constant variety, $i.\,e.$, in intensity. "The capacity of willing is a power absolute in its own arbitrament," says L. P. Hickok.

Dr. Strong does not make the essential distinction between constraint, and personic action. He places the will under the law of cause and effect, and denies it the power of alternative choices.

According to his teaching, the will can neither create nor originate moral character, for it is constrained in its activities. He indeed makes what he calls the occasional cause the real cause of all our volitions. The occasional cause is the motive or reason in view of which the will acts. He only mentions the efficient cause, as it appears to me, to avoid shocking the universal religious consciousness of our moral liberty. He inserts the causality of a volition into a mere passive motive, which is simply offered to the consideration of a sovereign being, for his acceptance or his rejection. Good and bad motives must come into comparison in the choices of every free agent, or he can possess no alternative action which is essential to personality. It is in choosing between conflicting feelings, that millions are constantly being saved or lost for eternity. To deny this proposition is to deny not only sovereign logic, but also all energizing theology. "All action is not necessary. We have *power* over our actions which dispense rewards and punishments," says Ralph Cudworth.

Dr. Strong says, "The will can choose any thing not inconsistent with its previous preferences." But what was it that caused " the previous preference?" Who is accountable for that preference? Was it a constrained preference? Underneath the writings of all the advocates of fore-ordination or of foreknowledge lurks the fatal and monstrous fallacy, that the human will acts under the law of cause and effect even in responsible action. It is, therefore, controlled by objective circumstances or subjective habits or sensibilities, and is not in itself sovereign. But the will, in its responsible choices, never acts under the law of constraint, but always under the law of liberty and of the power of contrary choices. Upon this simple and only point hangs the possibility of human accountability, of moral achievement, of reward, of punishment, and also of God's complacent delight and happiness in his intelligent creatures. "Every man is capable of either virtue or of vice," said Justin Martyr, one of the most authoritative of the fathers.

Dr. Strong says, "An action without a motive is irrational." True, but a choice between opposing motives is not irrational, but it is eminently rational, for without opposing motives a rational choice is simply impossible. It seems to me that it indicates a lack of discrimination, to dub the responsible action of a person with the cognomen of spontaneity. Spontaneity expresses the sensitive and constraining elements, but lacks the rational and original elements. The term arbitrariness, used by some to express personic action, seems to me to be open to several objections. It seems to exclude rationality, and that naturalness which ought to attach to the action of a responsible being. It seems also to suggest, that the consideration or impulse of the action, is mere stubbornness or foolhardiness. The term supernatural, the favorite of Bushnell and others, seems to be so liable to be misapprehended when any meaning at all is apprehended, that this action, I prefer to express by the term personic, or godlike. Indeed, I would prefer to call it personic-godlike, for then the definition would have two eyes, one looking down into the unmeasured depths of personality, and the other looking up to the unmeasured depths of the infinite Model. It also appears to me that in every case of deliberate responsible action, the alternate conflicting motives, to the seeming of the actor at the moment of test, are precisely equal in strength. This seems to me to be absolutely indispensable, if we allow to self-hood, responsible self-hood, a perfect arena on which to show its self-hood, to achieve character, to display loyalty, to indicate merit, and to exhibit reason for reward. It is then able to hold itself in *equilibrium*, and act for or against the motives presented from its mere determination to do so. "Deferment of choice is not choice," says Dr. Miley; " it is an immanent power of rational self-action, essential to personality. Reciprocal complacency in character between man and man or between man and angel or between man and God, can have no possible existence save in the free origination of congenial moral feelings. A person can originate a persistent disposition in his spirit that may control any urgency of sense. Moral worthiness is of significance only so far as it has been produced by an act that is simply internal. It is formed purely by internal decisions."

Dr. Strong says, "We require men to choose from reasons, not without reasons." True, but they cannot choose from reasons without at the same moment choosing against reasons. Trial always implies *pro* and *con* reasons. He says, "Only as there is a motive behind the deed is an agent responsible." True, but he cannot be responsible unless he refuse to yield to one motive and choose to yield to its competitor. He says, " Power to do what one does not desire is impotence." How, then, does he explain the reformation of the adulterer? He is chained by his brazen fetters of lust. God gives him power to choose what he does not desire, and, therefore, he appeals to his fears. Jesus has restored to him the power of self-determination, and self-determination presupposes possibilities which may or may not be realized.

If a sinner cannot, through proffered grace, recover himself voluntarily from his iniquity, then either the atonement was entirely useless, or no holy being ever could apostatize from his first estate. If my will is so controlled by my depraved desires that I cannot, through proffered prevenient grace, change from my sinful purposes, then Adam's will was so controlled by his holy desires that he could not change from his holy purposes. True, I am a fallen being, but through the great atonement the grace necessary to my regeneration is *congenital* with me, and is ever ready to co-operate with me.

Dr. Strong says, "Man cannot choose to love God and holiness." But is not every man empowered so to do by the Holy Ghost in virtue of the atonement? Did not the great atonement free and ransom all men from the necessary control of inborn depravity? Did it not restore all men to a state of moral freedom, and did it not place the entire race in a state of salvability? If it did not, then the glorious missions of the Redeemer and of the Holy Spirit were only mournful failures in the great enterprise of redemption. All of God's assumptions in calling sinners to repentance are, therefore, utterly groundless.

In one sense man is not free to choose good, because through the fall he became utterly depraved. In another sense man is free to choose good, because Christ redeemed him, and graciously gave to him power to freely choose the good. In one sense man is not free to choose sin, because awful penalties await him. In another sense he is free to choose sin, because it is only in the exercise of his freedom that he can achieve moral worthiness. In human volition there is one element that depends on God, and another element which depends on man. The element in volition which depends on man must be independent of God, or God is the author of sin, a conclusion too dreadful to entertain. Human guilt can have no basis but self-decision. Sin has its origin in an intelligent act of freedom.

Dr. Strong does not distinguish between character and the results of character on the intellect and the sensibilities, illuminating the mind and changing the moral qualities of the soul. In saying that the inward affections constitute the character, he overlooks the distinction between character and the moral nature. Character can only be achieved by the will. It can only be the result of the free choices of a free-will acting under the law and power of contrary choices. God can make souls and worlds, but he cannot make for his creatures a character that can justly be rewarded or punished. "Nothing can be virtuous," said Dr. Reid, "but that which is voluntary." "There can be no holiness," said Joseph Cook, "without freely choosing to love what God loves, and to hate what God hates."

Free choices, so soon as put forth, carry, according to the law of cause and effect, moral qualities and feelings and views and longings correspondent to these choices down into all the sensibilities. Washington's moral character, to which Dr. Strong refers as being incorruptible, was made by Washington himself. In lieu of a lofty, he might have achieved a degraded character. This he might have done with precisely the same mental and moral functions, the same outward surroundings and the same inward aspirations, *i. e.*, conflicting aspirations. Without the slightest change in his environments he might have made himself worse than Benedict Arnold. If he could not have betrayed his country, then for not betraying it he deserves no praise. Without making a deliberate choice between perfidy and patriotism, he could not have won the brightest name in the annals of fame.

But, according to the views and philosophy of Dr. Strong, how was it possible for sin ever to invade a sinless soul? But sin did invade sinless souls. It invaded the souls of the angels that kept not their first estate; sin entered into them in all defiance of the law, the wishes, the plans, and notwithstanding the unutterable grief of God. This simple fact demolishes the whole theory of Dr. Strong, and leaves the earnest reader thereof peering, with feelings of dissatisfaction and of disappointment, into the mouth of a dark cave, from which he receives no comforting light to illumine his way on to his eternal destiny. This gentle "Atlas," with chaos on his shoulders, admits, with a heart-felt sigh, born of his perplexity, "I am not novice enough to believe that I can clear up all the dark places of this most intricate theme." To find mysteries in a religion revealed from heaven is what we might reasonably expect, for a religion without mystery would be a temple without Deity. But surely the ministers of our holy Christianity are not, therefore, authorized to demand from us faith in positive self-contradictions. Can good Dr. Strong think that a candid infidel seeking to know if there be truth in the Christian religion would not be embarrassed and enervated, if not offended even to resentment, at such an unphilosophical presentation of systematic theology as he has presented in these articles in the Review?

But, continues the doctor, "God chose one man to eternal life, not because of any thing in him, but for reasons which exist only in God." If this distressing dogma, this opinion of the unilluminated past, were true, how does Dr. Strong know it? And if it be true, what benefit can there be in its proclamation? All the warnings, proffers and promises of the Gospel can be faithfully proclaimed by the heralds of the cross without calling the least attention to an article of faith so suggestive of difficulties, that they will not be unobtrusive. And wherever it is proclaimed it uniformly fills the multitude with both resentment and indignation. Its proclaiming tends to lull into indifference all those who infer or fancy that they are among the chosen few, the elect from all eternity. Most certainly there can be urged no justifiable excuse or palliation for any longer exposing this forbidding and misshapen visage, wholly of man's creation, from out the pulpits of our Lord and Saviour Jesus Christ. Those pulpits were opened by the Redeemer of the world, to proclaim liberty to all captives, the acceptable year of the Lord, and the glad tidings of great joy to all people.

Calvinists have never been satisfied with the doctrine of unconditional decrees. They embrace that perplexing, confounding thought with the most inexpressible reluctance. They do it only because they deem that no admissible thought system has ever been presented to the republic of thinkers which is either explicable or defensible in its absence. But if God create a being capable of electing as he may sovereignly choose, no consideration has ever yet been conceived of, making it necessary for God to foreknow that choice. Divine foresight robs the author of a responsible act of all the needed inspiration to self-assertion which uncertainty alone can give. If the will cannot make a new commencement and mold its own determination, exclusive of all testing influences, it cannot be free.

"Here are two men," says Dr. Strong; "their

chances are the same, the grace offered them is the same; one accepts that grace, the other refuses it. One is saved, the other is lost. What makes them to differ in their decision and destiny? Their own free choice, replies the Arminian. And so not to God, but to man, is due the merit and glory of his salvation. And, accordingly, man elects, regenerates and sanctifies himself." Is it possible that the clear-minded Dr. Strong cannot distinguish between voluntarily surrendering sin and self, and merely accepting, through the help of the ever-present omnipotent grace, the proffered salvation, and the subsequent miraculous works of pardon, regeneration and sanctification? The divine conviction of sin and danger, the divine power to choose obedience, are amply given to each of these two individuals. This divine power each may exercise and be saved, or refuse to exercise, and be lost. If this be not true, then God is unjust enough to do more for the eternal salvation of one son than he will for another son.

While the soul is in the attitude of repentance, obedience and acceptance of the free gift, the Holy Spirit creates him anew in Christ Jesus. The will chooses holiness, and God makes the nature holy. Divine help is given to the will in all cases, whereby it can accept divine offers. This divine help, however, is not coercive in its action; it may be exercised or it may be neglected. All those who have definiteness in their religious experience must certainly be conscious of this fact.

The synergistic scheme does not, therefore, as

Dr. Strong affirms, "assume that man takes the initiative in his salvation." Through prevenient grace I can sovereignly choose to be holy, and then God can sovereignly choose to make me holy, on the condition of my choice and my faith. Where in this can there be a fiber or a ray of unevangelism? "A gracious free agency, a power of considering, reforming and coming to Christ," says John Fletcher, the famous author of the Checks, "is given through the atonement."

Dr. Strong says: "If I may have the power of contrary choices God cannot make it certain that we shall never fall." But the doctor has no proof that any one now on his probation will never fall. Temptation implies possibility of a lapse from righteousness. If it be now certain that A. will never fall, his probation is ended already. If it be certain that B. will never repent, then his probation has already terminated. Probation means an opportunity of choosing between life and death. And if it be now certain that B. will choose death, then it is the greatest unkindness to leave him any longer where he will not only injure all with whom he comes in contact, but will treasure up to himself wrath against the day of wrath. If it be now certain that he will be lost, why not spare him some of his immeasurable sufferings? What a profane insinuation is this upon the benevolence and parental tenderness of Deity! It is too bad, with the prescientist, to affirm that God now sees all this terrible certainty accumulating upon the destiny of B., and yet does nothing for its prevention.

But how can the affirmation that B. could not repent, and yet is left where he will inevitably add blackness to his darkness forever, be adequately anathematized? For its appropriate expression, the language of diabolism must surely be placed under contribution! "There are," says Dr. Strong, "ten thousand chances to one that, unkept by God, I shall fall and perish." But here he does not distinguish between choosing to keep ourselves and choosing to be kept by God. These two propositions differ as widely as darkness differs from light. "I was first shown," says Miss F. R. Havergal, "that the blood of Jesus cleanseth us from all sin—yes, from all sin—and then it was made plain to me that he who had thus cleansed me had power to keep me clean ; so that I utterly surrendered myself to him, and utterly trusted him to keep me. Before blessedness there must be surrender."

"But," says the doctor, "it is objected that, according to my teachings, Adam never could have sinned. I do acknowledge that there is a difficulty here which I cannot fully solve. Adam did really possess the power of contrary choices, the power of good and the power of evil at the same moment." If the redemption of Christ was of any benefit to human nature, if redeemed human nature is a thing different from depraved human nature, all men must possess the power of contrary choices. Jesus partially saves all men, "for he," it is written, "is the Saviour of all men," but especially the Saviour of all who believe in him.

"If any of Adam's descendants have the power of contrary choice," says the doctor, "they have it through divine grace, which puts into the soul dominant tendencies to holiness." But why should Dr. Strong insert this sentence, when he does not believe that any of Adam's descendants possess the power of contrary choice? He believes that neither the elect nor the reprobate can choose differently from that which they actually do choose. He says, "The grace that is given to us *makes* us will, and *makes* us will aright." But if God put dominant tendencies to holiness into the souls of some individuals, then in simply yielding to those "dominant" overcoming tendencies, moral character could not possibly be originated. If all died in Adam, and in Christ all are made alive, where can Dr. Strong discriminate? Did Jesus die for all? And what less can that mean than that enabling grace is given to all? "As in Adam all die, even so in Christ shall all be made alive."

"But," continues the doctor, "the power of contrary choice which was possessed by Adam was not the absurd nondescript faculty Arminians understand by that name. It was not the ability to decide without motives, or contrary to all motives. It was not a self-contradictory ability to choose that which we do not choose, or that which we do not on the whole want. Adam's choice of evil does not prove that he chose without motive, or contrary to motive. His choice does not, therefore, help the Arminians."

Now I do not by any means affirm that Adam

chose evil without any motive. Motives bearing on his will in an opposite direction were necessary to a choice. Not only motives, but also conflicting motives, attracting in alternate directions, are essential to all personic action. What can Dr. Strong mean by the "power to decide contrary to all motives?" If all the motives be in one way or from a single source, then there cannot be possibly any choice. "The power of contrary choice is not," he says, "the ability to choose that which we do not wish to choose." But a man wishes a watch which can be obtained by theft. On the other hand, he wishes to preserve his conscience and his integrity. He earnestly desires both these things, the watch and his integrity, and if, between these conflicting desires, he has not in his personality the personic power to decide averse to the theft, he cannot be accountable therefor. There is no place but in this independent personic action on which to posit our accountability. "The power of contrary choice does not imply," says the doctor, "ability to decide without motives or contrary to all motives." But Adam did not decide without motives. Motives to obey, and motives to disobey, were fully placed before him.

"But," says Dr. Strong, "the great difficulty is in understanding how a sinful motive could have found a lodgement in the heart of Adam. He chose evil, because he wanted to. How could he want to choose it? We cannot understand how the first unholy emotions could have found shelter in a mind fully set on God, or how temptations could overcome a soul without unholy propensities." Mere temptations to indulge unholy emotions and actually indulging the same are very different states. And, besides, such temptations to unholy emotions are essential to the creation of rewardability.

After granting to Adam the power of alternative choices, Dr. Strong has no warrant for the inference that his descendants do not possess the same essential power, from the simple fact that he is unable to trace the process through which it was possible for a sinless soul to revolt from his Creator. The necessity of denying to all the descendants of Adam the power of contrary choices does not exist anywhere, save in the requirements and logical sequences of the assumption of the doctrine of election and reprobation. Any metaphysical dust at this point is wholly unnecessary to those who reject that main feature of Calvinism. They believe that Jesus, in his infinite atonement, not only made a propitiation for the sins of the whole world and restored to fallen humanity its lost power of contrary choice, but, through the agency of the eternal Spirit, he incipiently regenerated universal human nature, up to that degree that would enable it to be responsive to the warnings of infinite love and the invitations of divine mercy.

The power of personic action is the universal consciousness of the race. It is a quality essential to a person. However fierce may be our temptation to a sinful deed, we all know that we possess the power sovereignly to choose the right and reject the wrong. And without this power the feeling of remorse would be impossible, unless God has endowed us with mendacious faculties. And if in man there were no power of personic action, how could we know that there is any such power in Deity? And if in him there is no power of personic action, he can possess no free-will; and if he have no free-will, the system of necessity binds him and binds all his universe in its merciless and endless chains.

Divine personality asserts itself continually, and human personality is constantly doing the same thing. "I spake unto thee in thy prosperity," said God, "but thou saidst, I will not hear. Surely then shalt thou be ashamed and confounded for all thy wickedness." But this definite personic action of which we are profoundly conscious, and which the Scriptures so amply teach, is all the explanation that is needed, or could be required, in reason, to account for the disobedience and fall of Adam from his state of sinlessness.

Had this one word been comprehended in all its heights and depths of meaning, the ponderous volumes written upon the subject would have been dispensed with as profitless for both authors and readers.

A writer in the March number of the "Princeton Review," 1881, iterates the hoary folly of the insolubility of the problem of moral evil. But simple personic action is the only requisite for the perfect solution of this long-mooted question. The personic action of choice between competing considerations as indispensable to accountability is axiomatic, and axioms can neither be proved nor disproved. Freedom is a simple idea, and therefore indefinable, for defining is separating a complexity into its simplicities. Freedom cannot be explained by empirical antecedents. Sin could have had its origin nowhere but in the personic action of the free-will of a rational and accountable creature. The personic action of self-hood is indispensable to the existence of sin. In all our scientific inquiries we are continually making assumptions which will enable us to explain unexplained phenomena. The only verification we ever can obtain for the truth of these assumptions is the fact, that by their aid we are enabled to establish order where confusion had previously reigned, and to arrive at invaluable scientific truths. We assume, for example, without proof and without the possibility of proof, that a body will continue in the state in which it is, whether of rest or of motion, unless acted upon by some external force. From this mere assumption we demonstrate the most important truths relative to all the motions in planetary worlds and throughout the stellar heavens. This same privilege and leverage cannot reasonably be denied to investigators of theological truths. Let us, then, assume as a basal truth that personic action, the indefinable power of alternate choices, is an attribute of mind, indispensable to personality, conscience, moral action, character and accountability. Just so soon as we do this the great problem of moral evil, the great enigmas of sin, suffering, degradation, remorse and innumerable woes, are all satisfactorily explained and accounted for. A free-will must certainly possess power to produce results morally unlike the nature or spirit of the person in whom that free-will resides. If this be not so, it would have been impossible for a pure soul ever to initiate disobedience. This power is the logical necessity, from its possession of the capability of freedom. A being who has not original power over his inward states and feelings, whatever they may be, cannot be a person, and as a person can never be treated and governed.

Free agency implies morality, and morality necessitates a free agency, positive, definite and clear all the way from the incipiency of a moral act to its final perpetration. Deny this and you will cause to disappear all the sublime significance from the human will. There can be no meaning to accountability, if accountable beings are not rewarded for obedience and punished for disobedience. It is impossible to conceive of a moral quality attaching to a being, without an opportunity is given him of achieving a good or a bad character. Some test must be instituted by which to determine whether right or wrong will be freely chosen. An accountable being must, therefore, be placed in a state or season of trial for him to demonstrate whether he will be obedient or disobedient, and whether he will love sin or holiness. Such a state is indispensable to the creation of moral character; to the display of loyalty to all that is good and of repugnance to all that is evil; to an unfolding of a capacity to enjoy God and all his glorious rewards; to an exhibition of merit or demerit to witnessing worlds; to the manifestation of a claim on the favor of God, or of a desert of his awful frown. It is indispensable for the endless missions of glory and renown through interminable years, awaiting the loyal and the obedient. But to achieve moral desert there must be seeming difficulties in the way of obedience, and seeming facilities in the way of disobedience. Personic action implies a person, and a choice is essential to personality. A susceptibility to the appeal of motives, in the soul of the tested, is essential to his trial. A fair choice, a choice creative of moral character, is impossible without *pro* and *con* incentives. Incentives to obedience and incentives to disobedience are the essential conditions of a choice between them. Incentives to obedience must not, however, be so attractive as to overpower the actual capacities of the individual will, and thus completely overthrow its power of free choice. Visions of the glory of God, the transports of immediate bliss, or the horrors of instant banishment into outer darkness, could be presented so vividly to the susceptibilities of any man as to make it impossible for him deliberately and freely to originate a choice that could by any means involve moral worth or moral desert.

I choose to keep my feet out of the fire, but such a choice could not create moral character. In such a case there could not be any ground for a choice that could be worthy of reward. Instinctive promptness in rejecting temptations precludes the possibility of any genuine test of merit or of demerit. Without powerful and conflicting incentives between which to choose, the evolving of moral worthiness is simply impossible.

On the other hand, the incentives to disobedience must be neither too weak nor too strong. If they are too strong, the will has not a fair chance or trial, and cannot, therefore, of itself sovereignly determine, but is overborne by influences out of proportion to its ability to withstand or endure. If these incentives, on the other hand, are too weak, inconsiderable or forceless, then there could not be a basis broad enough, rational, deliberate and sensitive enough, in which to originate a choice which could be creative of moral desert, or evincive of untrammeled free agency and of personality. These incentives to obedience and these incentives to disobedience, must, therefore, be graduated in exact proportion to the ability of the endurance of each individual will. These opposing incentives must also be equalized, and their equality ever maintained by the infinite Tester, or the pure creation of moral acts is impossible to man. The *pro* and *con* incentives, competing for personic action, must, to the individual undergoing the test, ever appear to be equal. Were this not the case, self-hood could not, untrammeled, virtuously or viciously assert itself. If the incentives for one of two alternatives appear to the individual to be stronger for one than for the other, then the will might not be able to rest in the equilibrium indispensable for personic action, and for the creation of moral character. If the incentive for one alternate be stronger than the incentive for the other alternate, and the choice must go with that s ronger incentive, then it is not the person that chooses, but the incentive that coerces him. Without these incentives to obey and to disobey, an arena on which choices can be made, originative of rewardability or punishability, can never be found nor even conceived of. But the incentives to obey must always be veiled in their nature and reality, and limited in their number, weight and impressiveness, or they would necessarily disturb the valid conditions of choice, and defeat all the great purposes of probationary state. If their reality and splendor and immeasurable worth were not largely veiled, a choice displayful of moral character, demonstrative of merit, or indicative of demerits, or originative of personal worth, would be impossible.

The sole object of probation is to afford accountable beings an opportunity of originating for themselves moral worthiness or unworthiness. Over the many incentives to obedience, therefore, there must of necessity be thrown shadow enough, uncertainty enough, and seeming dubiety enough, to afford the tested person a fair judicial opportunity of exercising his personic action.

On the other hand, the incentives to disobedience, however illusory, deceptive and unreasonable they in truth are, must, nevertheless, be presented to the mind of the probationer under such a veil of concealment and with such a semblance of reality and under such an aspect of attractiveness, as really to seem desirable realities, promissory of gratification, with no very serious obstacles in the way of a return to obedience and of escaping the hideous consequences of disobedience.

Without such a presentation of reality, attractiveness and plausibleness in the hollow incentives held out for disobedience, a choice evincive of merit would be impossible and inconceivable in the very nature of things. A sinful motive, clothed with all the seeming reality, must be presented as a consideration for the understanding to contemplate and as an attraction for the sensibilities to realize, in order that a person may have an opportunity of freely, deliberately, and sovereignly choosing to resist downward attractions and temptations, and to make a choice creative of moral character. In no other way could a sinless person originate a choice worthy of reward or worthy of punishment. To be a free spirit, holy or unholy, he must, as we have said, possess the power to originate acts morally unlike himself. If he cannot do this he cannot be a person. The possibility of heaven evidently implies the possibility of hell. "I am glad," exclaimed one, "that I can do wrong, for if I could not do wrong I could not do right." The power of creating holy character implies the power of creating an unholy character. Ability to do what God commands implies ability to do what God forbids. A sinful motive, then, must move on the susceptibilities in order to test the firmness and endurance of the will and to bring out the capability of the will in positiveness either in holiness or unholiness.

Without the free exercise of the untrammeled

power of choice between opposing incentives or competitive motives, moral character and moral deserts can never be achieved or even conceived of. These alternative incentives must, therefore, wear deceptive impressiveness. The reality and glory of the incentives to obedience must be greatly dimmed and diminished or they would render impossible the legitimate conditions of choice. The unreality, delusiveness and danger of the incentives to disobedience must be veiled beneath a drapery of fascination and reality, or they too would defeat all the purposes of probation by eliminating all moral significance from moral choices. The three and four times degrading nature of sin must be obscured into apparent twilight in order to produce the hesitation and deliberate action necessary to a choice evincive of worthiness. The delight promised in the indulgence of sin must be so intense as to make a deep impression upon all the susceptibilities of the being who is under trial for eternity. The test of a pure being, by which to evolve rewardability or punishability or moral character, without the reality of the great and various incentives to obedience being in some way lessened and obscured, and without the deceptive incentives to disobedience being in some way made interesting and charming, is simply all utter inconceivability. But these deceptive impressions, which are so indispensable in furnishing an arena on which man's pure personality can assert and manifest itself, arise in the process of temptations addressed to the soul on its probation by the wicked one.

The sacred Scriptures teach us that Satan tempts, deceives, persuades, animates, leads, blinds, captivates, threatens, and diligently sows the seeds of death, while making the most glowing promises of early and splendid fruitions. He misleads us as to such things as the profits and the pleasures to be derived from the anticipated sinful gratification; the real sinfulness or turpitude of the wicked deed in contemplation; the dreadful results of disobedience; the difficulties in the way of return to the divine favor after transgression; the loss of self-respect, and the bitter agonies of self-condemnation.

These views of the incentives which compete for our obedience or our disobedience, for our independent suffrage, are necessary to a test that would be adequate to meet all the conditions necessary to our accountability, and which could evolve out of our personality rewardableness or punishableness, and the splendors of an achieved moral character. Without such views, an arena where loyalty to the truth, to God, and to self can be displayed is inconceivable. But with these views carefully considered, the whole process of the fall from sinlessness is as simple as any necessary truth itself. These views furnish the real factors and conditions of a probation that has in it any aim, object, significance or genuine reality. Without them probation for eternity is not only meaningless and realityless, but even farcical and useless. These views do present the conditions necessary to a possibility of self-denial, of self-control, of undergoing something for the sake of the truth, of preferring duty to gratification, of believing in lieu of doubting the divine prohibitions and proffers, of deciding between obedience and disobedience, of resting on the fairness of divine dealings, of obeying uncomprehended commandments, of deferring to the will of the universal Ruler, of living by faith, of walking trustfully in a valley where there is no light, and of stern adherence to the right amid powerful temptations to the wrong.

The possibilities of all these moral characteristics, all these indices of moral nature, lie wholly in the *pro* and *con* incentives placed before accountable beings, and which compete for their suffrage and adherence. Without such conflicting incentives as opposing forces struggling for the mastery of the person, the universe might have been filled with intelligent beings, but not one of them could ever have won the glorious distinction of personality; not one of them could ever have possessed the least moral character or moral desert or self-respect or individuality; not one of them could ever have enjoyed the consciousness that he had won for himself, in a fair fight, the respect of all holy beings, and the esteem, respect and confidence of his glorious Creator; not one of them could ever have enjoyed one thrill of happiness arising from the consciousness, " I was a valiant hero on the battlefields of probation for eternity;" not one of the countless millions could ever exclaim, "On my march from the cradle to the tomb I made a record and a history of dazzling magnificence. In my faith I never staggered; in my duty I never flinched; in my development I never wearied; and in my loyalty I never wavered." The innocent, characterless, deservingless, personless, forceless multitudes would have been no more to Jehovah than so many flowers or gems or stars or senseless soulless things. And the transcendent idea of the rewards of moral valor could never have been conceived of from everlasting unto everlasting. Never, never, could that splendid thought have dawned upon the human intellect or entranced an intelligent universe.

This was the probation in which Adam fought and sadly failed. It was the same in which the fallen angels fought and kept not their first estate. This was the probation in which the man Christ Jesus, as a pure human consciousness, in his pure created personality, fought and most gloriously triumphed, irradiating all worlds with the effulgence of his triumphs. This is the probation of every accountable being now upon the earth. The lapse and disobedience of Adam are no more mysterious than the disobedience of any one of his descendants. Any act of sinful disobedience of any living man is just as mysterious, and no more enigmatical, than the fall of Adam. "Nothing but mean thoughts are mysterious to me," said Edward Irwing. No explanation of the fall of Adam can be required, save his possession of the personic power of choice, which was essential to his personality.

After writing the above, great was my gratification in reading the following from the revered Francis Wayland: "Our first parents were endowed with moral powers, capable of appreciating their obligations to their Creator, and with an intellect by which they became aware of the consequences of their actions. All the conditions which were necessary to influence their decision were within the sphere of their vision, and they were endowed with unrestrained liberty of choice. The trial to which they were subjected was by no means unreasonable for beings thus endowed. The preponderance of motives was, as might naturally be expected, to lead them to choose the path of virtue and happiness. The word of the tempter was set against the word of the Creator. A momentary sensual gratification was opposed to the displeasure of the eternal Father. The finite was put in comparison with the infinite. It was under such circumstances that man was required to hold fast his integrity during the brief period of his probation, with the promise, if he were found faithful, of immortal felicity. The result was left dependent upon man's free-will. After all he is, and from the necessity of his nature he must be, liable to sin. He may act in opposition to every noble and generous motive, and yield himself up to the seductions of sense. Unless there existed this liability he could not be capable of virtue or vice. Do you ask how he could sin? This question may be answered in no other manner than by an appeal to the consciousness and to the observation of any man. Why is it that we see such things done every day? Why is it that every thoughtful man feels himself liable continually to just such moral disaster? Why is it that men, by a single vicious indulgence or the gratification of a single unholy desire, cover themselves with infamy?"

But really the motive that was presented to Adam through which to test his loyalty was an incentive to indulge in an object which was sinless in itself. It was an object that, had it not been forbidden, might have been enjoyed, and with the divine blessing upon it. Its gratification was sinful only because it had been positively prohibited. An incentive, or temptation to indulge in that which was wicked in itself, might have made him so shudder as to retreat before the trial of his strength was brought on. Such a suggestion might have been manifestly so hideous and pregnant of evil as to preclude the possibility of a test which could have been evincive of moral achievement. For me to resist the suggestion to commit murder could be no evidence of my loyalty to God; so a motive to positive wickedness might have been so incongruous and shocking to a sinless nature as to prevent his putting forth volitions worthy of divine reward and self-respect. But to indulge in the enjoyment of a thing lawful in itself could not have appeared so alarming as to defeat all the great purposes of a probation for eternity. Adam's sin was really in obtaining a thing good in itself, but which had been divinely forbidden. Had God more fully illumined his mind; could he, with a clearer and a broader vision, have seen the consequences of his contemplated sin; could he have seen virtue in all its unspeakable attractions promptly, he would have rejected all the fascinations spread out before his eyes, those which were addressed to his instinctive love of beauty, to his desires of knowledge and power, and those whispered in his ear by a malignant and wily foe. But, under such excesses of illumination, his decision, his choice of obedience, and his final determination would have been no evidence at all of loyalty to truth, duty and God. They could not have been creative of his moral character, nor could they have furnished any reason why he should be divinely rewarded. From a choice made under such excessive illumination there could have resulted no high excellence of soul, and no realization of the great ends of probation. For the realization of such ends he needed to be placed, where, in order to show his loyalty, he must resist unholy influences, maintain harmony and purity in his affections, stand trustfully and obediently amid the incentives to do wrong and the incentives to do right, and in triumph pass all the assaults made upon his integrity. The illusory but seemingly real incentives to disobedience needed to be strong enough to afford him an adequate test, a fair trial, but not in the least to exceed his capacities of endurance, or in the least to constrain his choice. But, notwithstanding all the incentives to disobedience, all the blinding and deceptive attractiveness of contemplated gratifications, without the deliberate consent and choice of his will, they could not have disturbed the proper action and equilibrium of the sensibilities of his soul. However strong the temptations that assailed him, they would have been harmless but for the consent of his will. It was in the free, but wrong, exercise of this faculty that his demerit consisted.

When his will sovereignly chose to yield to an improper and abnormal exercise and impulse of his sensibilities, a moral disturbance was at once introduced among those sensibilities, a disturbance which broke down the harmony and unsettled the relations which God had instituted between them, a disturbance which finally perverted and reversed the whole action of the moral sensibilities of his soul.

If the sinless sensibilities be once gratified beyond the limits expressly permitted by the Creator, it would in some slight degree generate emotional disorder, mental depreciation and volitional wavering.

When a disturbance of the sensibilities was really effected, a state of sinfulness passed down into the essence of the soul, and total depravity was the necessary result. It was in this way that moral evil stole into the heart of the first man. How long the trial lasted, how frequent the onsets, how many the battles, how dreadful the struggles, ere the sensibilities lost their balance, ere moral evil gained allowance in his soul, we can never know. But all that is required to explain his fall and the origin of evil is a comprehension of the single term, personic action, by which I mean power to determine, unbiased by impulses.

By the term original sin we may mean the innate bias, bent or tendency of any human being to sin.

This is accounted for in the fact that we are the children of a fallen father and included in the covenant of redemption. But the term original sin may refer to the primal sin of Adam, introducing moral evil into our world. Of the origin of this primal sin Jonathan Edwards never attempts an explanation. All his works center around the relations of man to grace. When God made man he made him with sinless susceptibilities and sinless sentiments. He endowed him with a nature sinless in itself and without any but holy affinities. But moral perfection means more than this. It includes moral character, which could only be superadded by freely volitionating in harmony with the standard of absolute rightness. A sinless moral nature, including sinless susceptibilities and sinless views, and the possibility of moral evil, were wholly without sinful prepossessions or tendencies. God could not have achieved a moral character for Adam, and, therefore, he could not have given to him moral perfection.

Moral freedom means power to do good or power to do evil. If it does not mean that, it is a most provoking *ignis fatuus*. Power to do evil must necessarily have its origin apart from God. "The line of contact between the human will and the divine agency can never be drawn," said Dr. D. Curry. But surely we can discriminate the line where divine agency goes and the human will self-operates in matters of sin. If man's power to do evil must needs have its origin apart from God, then also his power to do good must equally have its origin apart from God. If you deny this you rob him of, or blot out from him, one half of his personality. A being who possesses these two distinct powers apart from God must necessarily be a person, and not a machine or mere instrument. It was simply impossible, therefore, for God to have endowed man with moral perfection. Had man started with moral perfection there could have been no possibility of moral evil. But such a start and an endowment we have seen were impossible and self-contradictory. The origin of sin is the possibility implied in freedom. "The origin of sin," said Julius Mueller, "is an ideal or intelligible self-perversion of free-will." Moral perfection could only be brought about by free self-determination. A man, therefore, may have a holy soul and yet will sinfully. That God would have prevented sin had it been possible for him to have done so is a postulate we must never surrender. "As to the origin of moral evil," says Dr. Daniel Curry, "the greatest intellects are beyond their depths." But the great Guizot says: "The fact of original sin presents nothing strange, nothing obscure; it consists essentially in disobedience to the will of God, which will is the moral law of man. This disobedience, the sin of Adam, is an act committed everywhere and every day, arising from the same causes, marked by the same character, and attended by the same consequences, as the Christian dogma assigns to it. At the present day, as in the Garden of Eden, this act is occasioned by a thirst for absolute independence, the ambitious aspirings of curiosity and pride, or weakness in the face of temptation." "He destroys the idea of development altogether who regards a settled moral state as the original one for man, the prius, and looks upon every moral act and decision as the necessary outgo and effect of this settled state," said Julius Mueller.

Even the Arminian lantern which, one hundred and fifty years since, Bishop Butler hung up in this murky valley, would have afforded light sufficient to illumine this question, with all its corollaries, if the attachment to human creeds and established formulas had not been so excessive and conservative. But the psychological light that now shines upon this subject is as bright, clear, animating and refreshing as that which fell from the mysterious star and illumined the rugged way of Eastern sages in their weary search after the infant Redeemer. Why, then, should the fall of man any longer be denominated the mystery of mysteries?

"But," says Dr. Strong, "the power of choice does not explain an unholy choice." Yes, but man possesses not only power but personic choice, and if personality does not involve power essential to originate choices, holy or unholy, all comprehension or settlement of theology must be adjourned beyond the day of judgment. "It is the blackest of blasphemies," says Dr. Strong, "to affirm that God created any finite being with original dispositions to evil." He is fully entitled to utter this invective after granting to Adam the power of contrary choice, the power to do good and the power to do evil at the same moment. But granting to Adam the power of alternate choices, and then denying the same to his redeemed and incipiently regenerated descendants, seems to me to remove all the foundations of his theology, and leave it whistling in the wild winds of infidelity.

How long must our glorious Christianity be disfigured and dishonored by such enervating and unscriptural teachings, and that, too, from out her most respectable pulpits? It is sad to think how much time, learning, genius and piety have been wasted in attempts at explaining manifest absurdities and in defending indefensible positions. It is enough to change the gladdest angel into a Jeremiah to behold profound and devout men, sent with a divine commission to open the prison doors to them that are bound and to preach the acceptable year of the Lord, devoting their energies in herculean efforts to clothe evident follies in robes of reason, or to make a provoking absurdity wear the countenance of an angel of light. Dr. R. M. Patterson, of Philadelphia, in the late Pan-Presbyterian Council said: " Let us never forget in our work our settled belief that God's work will be done in his own time, in his own way, and to the extent to which he has himself determined." Such teachings cannot fail to dampen the fires of zeal, excuse from painful, pinching, personal sacrifices, check the origination of moral forces, render listless all individual inquiries for new moral enterprises in the name of the Lord, lull men into indifference over the waste places of Zion, and paralyze all the self-originating energies of majestic faith and prevailing prayer. No one can read in the "Princeton Review," number for July, 1880, of the fifty-fourth year, the article on God's indiscriminate proposals of mercy and salvation, as related to divine sincerity, from the pen of Dr. Robert L. Dabney, of Hampden Sydney Theological College, Va., without sighing over the wasted energies, squandered talents, misapplied learning and misused time of a really good, strong and genuine man. His struggles of thought and far-reachings, his filling up gaps of logic with heroic affirmations, his rushing by difficulties, cap in hand, lest he should see them, his bewrayed conscious quiverings and quakings of soul, and his sibyllic contortions, can create in his readers nothing but alternate pity, mirth and sadness.

Dr. Robert Hall speaks of Dr. Howe as "the wonderful Howe," and declares that "his masterpiece of thought and reasoning is his effort to reconcile the divine sincerity with the offers of life and salvation so freely made to the eternally reprobate." Dr. Dabney, in the article above referred to, struggling on the Calvinistic platform to defend the character of God from the charge of insincerity in offering salvation to reprobates, says: "He indeed would be a rash man who should flatter his readers that he was about to furnish an exhaustive explanation of the mystery of the divine will. But any man who can contribute his mite to a more satisfying and consistent exposition of the Scriptures bearing upon it is doing a good service to truth."

We will now explain what Dr. Dabney refers to in the phrase "mystery of the divine will" upon the influence and workings of grace in regenerating the soul of man. John Calvin fastened his mechanical conception of the mode of the action of material forces upon the workings of grace. He looked upon the grace of God and mechanics as perfectly analogous in their operation. For this fundamental error his profound mind was in no way censurable. This view was perfectly consistent with the false but generally received psychology of his times. The then prevalent philosophy made the will a mere sensibility, and, therefore, necessarily under the rigorous law of cause and effect. From this fatal misconception clothing the modality of grace with constrained modality of mechanical philosophy, the irresistibility of grace was an inevitable conclusion which could not possibly be gainsaid. With the irresistibility of grace as a premise, a limited atonement, election and reprobation and final perseverance of the elect, were logically unavoidable and necessary as fate itself. Grace, in the view of Calvin, being the efficient cause, *per se*, always produces its effect, and can never, never be defeated in its action. All, therefore, for whom Christ died will be saved, and no others can be. Hence Calvin declared, "Christ redeemed only those who were chosen to salvation from eternity." From this it was inevitable that the redemption of the race was only partial. But as the Bible offers salvation indiscriminately to all, Calvin saw no way to extricate himself from the tremendous difficulty but by discriminating between a revealed divine will, which offered salvation to all men, and a secret divine will, which nullified and defeated the revealed divine will, which offered salvation to all. The mystery of the divine will to which Dr. Dabney refers is, then, the awful mystery of a dualistic will in God relative to a fallen world, electing some to eternal life and leaving the rest to perish forever. But what is Dr. Dabney's "mite" for elucidating this great mystery of the divine offers of life to all while provision was made only for a part. He says: "The words, 'God so loved the world,' mean, and were intended to express, a divine propension of benevolence, not, however, matured into a volition to redeem. God does have compassion upon reprobates, but he does not possess a volition to save them. God's *touching* appeals to the non-elect are evidences of true compassion, which are, however, restrained by consistent and holy reasons from taking the form of a volition to regenerate them. For God does compassionate those whom he never proposed to save or promised to save. God does, through Christ, make sincere offers of mercy to sinners, and when that offer is slighted, as it was *permissively decreed that it should be*, he illustrates his *justice* by destroying them."

When I had read these strange statements from an acknowledged prophet of the Lord in the nineteenth century I could hardly credit the report of my eyes. I was intellectually amazed and bitterly pained through all the realm of my sensibilities, and I cried out, in the language of Jeremiah, "I am black; astonishment hath taken hold on me." I then naturally inquired if the earlier statements and teachings of Calvinists were as open to the honest criticism of candid inquirers for the truth, sitting beneath the cross of an atoning Christ. I then found emblazoned upon the pages of the good and distinguished Dr. E. D. Griffin the following most perplexing hand-writing: "In the ages of eternity a covenant was formed between the persons of the sacred Trinity, in which the Father made over to his Son a definite number of the human race, as a reward of his obedience unto death, and caused their names to be written in the Lamb's book of life. For God actually *forces* a part of the human family to heaven. And he does this for just as many as the interests of the universe will permit." Here I unconsciously ejaculated with King David, "Let us fall now into the hand of the Lord; for his mercies are great: and let me not fall into the hand of man."

After defending predestination and striving to reconcile the universal offers of life to reprobates with the sincerity of God, Dr. Hill remarks: "It is, however, difficult to reconcile the mind to a system that denies saving grace to such multitudes. A very dark cloud, therefore, hangs over the whole subject." And Dr. Thomas Chalmers, in his attempted solution of this great perplexity of freely offering eternal life to those who were not elected thereunto, mournfully admits, in the tumultuous tenderness of his great soul, "There certainly must be some sad fundamental misunderstanding upon the whole subject somewhere." How the declaration of Calvin, that God makes his call universal, but "he directs his voice to the reprobates that they may become more deaf, he kindles a light for them that they may be made more blind and besotted," must have distressed the great heart of Chalmers! "These words of Calvin," exclaimed Bledsoe, "made my blood run cold." They are as shocking as the declaration of Augustine, " Infants dying unbaptized will certainly be damned." One not fortified by prepossessions would be likely to see that the perplexing mystery lies in embracing a theology that really, in the final fact, necessitates the constraint of the human will, and still holds over it the retribution of eternity.

"There is," says Dr. Chalmers, "a deep theology within the soul which answers to the theology taught in the Scriptures." There is not one man in gospel-illumined lands who does not know that Jesus died for him, ascended for him, and now calls for him. Every man feels, in the depths of his consciousness, that his endless destiny is suspended upon his own will in repenting of sin and willingly accepting the free gifts of pardon and regeneration through the merits of the atonement. If this is not true, then "the grace of God that bringeth salvation hath not appeared unto all men," nor is it true that the light of Jesus enlighteneth "every man that cometh into the world." Jesus was manifested to destroy the works of the devil, and the Holy Ghost was manifested "to convince the world of sin, of righteousness and of a judgment to come." Therefore the deep theology within teaches that all through Jesus Christ have the offer and the opportunity of eternal salvation. And this answers exactly to the freeness and universality of the terms of the Gospel.

Thus we evidently see that there is no election and reprobation in the deep religious consciousness of the world. And, Calvinian Chalmers being judge, there can be none in the Bible. " Deep calleth unto deep." The deep theology within answers to the deep theology without. And the deep theology without answers to the deep theology of universal Christian consciousness. But the foundations of Calvinism were never laid in the Bible. Not one of its five points or main features was ever, as I have noted, referred to but to be condemned and reprobated by the apostles and their successors, the fathers, for the first four hundred years of the Christian era. The foundations of Calvinism were laid by honest men in the shifting sands of a false and long-since repudiated psychology. Public opinion has chased the dogma of sovereign eternal election and reprobation out of general acceptance and respectability. Of the Scripture apparent strongholds of this tenet of Calvinism, one after another is being abandoned by the ripest and devoutest Calvinistic scholars themselves. All that is needed to keep it from embarrassing the coming generations of theologians is to dislodge it from its erroneous metaphysics. This, in love, earnestness and prayer, with a single eye to the glory of God, I have tried to accomplish.

But Calvinism teaches also that, though I am not conscious that I sinned in Adam's apostasy, nevertheless I am responsible for that apostasy, and, though I am unable to repent of that sin, nevertheless its guilt is imposed upon me. I have none of Adam's personality, none of his consciousness, none of his struggles with the dark forms of sin, none of his pungent convictions for sinning in the garden, and none of his biting remorse; nevertheless I did, according to Calvinistic teachings, participate in that sin, and do now share its dreadful guilt. But, then, are not these manifest contradictions? How can I be guilty without the consent of my will, without the remorse that follows willful transgression, and without any power to repent of the sin? And how could I be guilty of the sins of one predecessor without being guilty of the sins of all predecessors? I can inherit all these consequences of Adam's sin, guilt excepted, because I am indissolubly connected with him in well-being and in destiny. If I did not inherit these guiltless consequences of Adam's wickedness the dreadful nature of sin would be greatly lessened and obscured. These disadvantages, these degrading consequences of sin, following invariably upon the whole race, constitute great restraints and educating forces upon individuals and communities. It is the impossibility that personal guilt can attach to any but a conscious violation of law that triumphantly establishes the all-important doctrine of individualism, and makes each soul a splendid unit standing in his greatness and also in his awful responsibility before the Judge Eternal. I know that I am an accountable being to be considered and treated in my pure individuality because I, and I alone, am capable of personal guilt. For myself, I am a unit in my individuality, and for the race, I am a fractional part, and must necessarily suffer or shine with it to a very large extent and as to very many particulars. Without the guiltless consequences of sin upon the race collectively, there could be no corporate unity or solidarity; and without a corporate unity of the race there could be no great world-plans carried on and up into ideal realizations. In the interpretations of these vast problems we need a vivid recognition of God's great world-purposes. For, besides his plans embracing the future and eternal existence of souls as individuals bound to account before a future tribunal, he has, doubtless, many temporal plans for our world illustrative of his wisdom and power and his other boundless resources. He seems to delight in wheels within wheels, and, indeed, infinitely varied rays of light streaming from every spoke in those wheels. But of these important distinctions both Augustine and Calvin had conceptions the most limited and confused; and these confused and meagre conceptions have been perpetuated among their adherents to this hour. Dr. Dorner says: "To Augustine, Adam was a double amphibological notion which seeks to combine in thought irreconcilable factors. He taught that all Adam's posterity participated in his guilt and are liable to his punishment. He does not, therefore, think that it is unjust that heathen and unbaptized heathen should be lost. The Old Testament does not favor the rigid doctrine of original sin. The importance of this question is very great, as on its decision depends whether we are committed to absolute predestination or whether a place remains for human freedom and human responsibility." Page 332, vol. ii. Calvinism rests on the bare desert of perdition for the sin of Adam. Guilt being the consciousness of having done wrong, can neither be inherited nor transmitted nor transferred. Indeed, the Calvinistic phrase, " imputed guilt," implies the innocence of him to whom guilt is imputed. The Scriptures nowhere teach that we are guilty of the sin of Adam, or that we are punished therefor. " They everywhere declare," says Dr. Wayland, " that every man is guilty simply of his own voluntary transgressions, and that the guilt of every man is to be estimated by the degree of moral light which he has voluntarily resisted." I was in Adam seminally but not individually, as the oak of to-day was in the oak of a hundred years ago.

The mist that has been thrown over this simple subject is truly amazing. Had Adam maintained his loyalty, his posterity would have stood upon a higher vantage ground. We instinctively perceive that this must have been God's ideal plan of race, elevation, and progression. But the moral character of each of Adam's descendants would have depended solely upon his own voluntary obedience.

The only ground of condemnation is the rejection of proffered light. But as Adam disobeyed and corrupted nature, and introduced into that nature a proneness to sin, his posterity must, according to that same ideal law, take a step downward to a less advantageous state, to a state of lower realizations. This was a state of great disadvantage and lessened opportunity, but it had in it not a single element of guilt. The guilt of each depended wholly upon his own voluntary disobedience. God's plan and his law in constituting the human race, were that a moral likeness should exist between parent and child. This was intended to be a powerful incentive to parental goodness and obedience. Adam, by his disobedience, having corrupted his nature, his child must necessarily resemble him in every particular save personal guilt. The incongruity of a morally unclean, unholy parent, being the progenitor of an offspring with no proneness to disobedience, would necessarily shock the moral sense of the moral universe. Reasons for this will readily occur to every thoughtful reader. The law of the necessity of moral resemblance in nature between parent and offspring must be observed and maintained for reasons numerous and impressive. When, therefore, man comes into the world, he comes necessarily as the child of a fallen father, with all the disadvantages of a fallen state, moral character only excepted. For no being but self can achieve a moral character for self. This proneness to sin is his inheritance, but his moral character is of his own creation, for that is the result of willing concordantly or discordantly with the moral standard lifted up for his conformity. No guilt can possibly attach to a proneness to sin for which man is in no way responsible, and of which he is in no sense the voluntary cause. Theologians have strangely carried the guilt of voluntary disobedience over to the passive state of a proneness to that disobedience. They ignored, or failed to see, that an energy was given to the will through the atonement to hold in check that proneness. Where sin abounds, under the Gospel, grace much more abounds. But this inherited state of proneness to sin, which in the nature of things was impossible to avoid, was partially lessened and modified by the redemption that is in Jesus Christ. Had no atonement been made, man would have been a helpless, hopeless demon. Christ by his death incipiently regenerated the human race up to the capacity of hearing the invitations of mercy and being saved. He lessened man's proneness to sin, restored to him his lost freedom, and sent the Holy Ghost to help all his infirmities. The blessings and advantages man lost in the disobedience of Adam by an inexorable law, were more than counterbalanced by the blessings and advantages obtainable through the atonement. I am unfortunate but not guilty in having a fallen father. I am infinitely fortunate in having an infinite Saviour and an infinite Sanctifier. "Original sin," says Dr. Dorner, "can only bear the character of a misfortune." P. 354. Julius Mueller defines " original sin to be the innate tendency or bias toward sinfulness in every human being." A darkened, fallen, sinward being needs redemption, but a personal guilt requires a personal, sinful volition. If guilt could be transmitted by generation, justice would imperiously require that the guilty pair be without progeny forever. In no other way could we shield divine goodness. God can look upon a nature unfortunately inclined to sin without attributing to it actual guilt. From our "inherited sinwardness" the Redeemer proffers to redeem us and preserve us and present us faultless before his Father's throne.

Thus a line of living light runs through this entire subject which has been so long and so strangely misconceived. Children come into the world not only innocent, but with a spiritual life communicated through the provisions of the atonement. "For as by one man's disobedience many were made sinners, so by the obedience of one shall many be made righteous." The spirituality lost to the race by Adam's transgression is restored to the race by Christ's obedience. But there is transmitted from parents to children a bias to wrong-doing which co-exists with their innocent spirituality and which develops into actual transgression when responsible life is reached. The Scriptures nowhere make inborn proneness to sin any excuse for voluntarily sinning against God.

I have mentioned this strange error as another of the vagaries with which Christianity should be no longer disfigured. But, strange to relate, the Presbyterian Church of Scotland has just re-affirmed that all mankind sinned in Adam, and therefor deserve divine wrath and punishment in time and in eternity. And thus is republished the monstrous dogma that men sinned ere they had an existence. "Do not," said a Calvinian minister to a young man going into the foreign missionary field, "do not speak of election until for years you have indoctrinated your Church." "I never speak of Calvinism in China," said Dr. Burns; "the Chinese do not need it." Surely the Church of the future ought not to be enervated by such untruthful, unreasonable, indeed, shocking doctrinal teachings. But no Calvinist can eliminate Adam's guilt out of his soul until he eliminates the appalling system of Calvinism out of the holy Oracles.

After Dr. Legge had been working for some time in Hong Kong, he thought the time had come for translating the Westminster Catechism. He called upon his native preacher to put it into Chinese. The work proceeded pleasantly until they came to the twentieth question, the answer to which is, "God, having out of his mere good pleasure from all eternity elected some to everlasting life, did enter into a covenant of grace to deliver them out of the estate of sin and misery and to bring them into an estate of salvation by a Redeemer." The preacher here threw down his pen, exclaiming, "I can't translate that."

"Why not?" inquired Dr. Legge.

"Because," said he, "we have been preaching that any body might come and be saved, and this says only those can come who have been elected. I can't translate this."

"Then," said Dr. Legge, "I put the Catechism upon a shelf, and there it stays."

Dr. Lyman Beecher, it is well attested, wore the system of Calvinism as a galling yoke for more than fifty years. Such a consciousness must feel the necessity of an extricator from such embarrassing tenets. Calvinism is now lying amid earthquakes with consternation in its face. We ought, therefore, to disembarrass the Church of all those doctrines and theories which have confessedly disfigured theology and paralyzed evangelical efforts. The study of Dr. Hodge's theology fully justifies the boast which he made to his assembled alumni that "No new idea ever originated in Princeton." With a fathomless Bible in our hands, a boundless ocean of divine truth heaving and breaking at our feet; and the incomprehensible Deity urging himself upon our devout and profound meditations, our discoveries and our fruitions, how could any mind which was not afraid of the breaking light of incoming truth through a better exegesis, a truer psychology and a more searching didactics, glory in such a narrow and unworthy boast? What! must the theological intellect be forever tethered to the errors, fallacies, ignorances, limitations and blinding prejudices, of a narrow, supercilious and persecuting past. That surely must be a pseudo-Christianity which quakes at a challenge for honorable combat in the forum of reason. "No one, however, is ever against reason except when reason is against him," says Bacon. But in the failure of revered old Princeton to satisfy her thinking sons, and to sweep out the floods of new views advancing upon their congregations, do we not see the necessity of some new theological teaching to bear up the ark of divine truth, steadily and grandly through all the storms and above all the waves of modern skepticism and rationalism?

Dr. Morris, of Lane Theological Seminary, lamented not long since in the "New York Evangelist" "the narrowness betrayed in the recent Pan-Presbyterian Council." That narrowness he thinks was evinced in many ways, such as "preventing a union communion service; excluding from the Council that noble band of Christian heroes, the Cumberland Presbyterians, because of their hesitation over the perplexing doctrines of election and reprobation; and trampling almost frantically upon the thoughts and sentiments of the progressive papers read by distinguished members of the body." He then affirms that "nothing but Christian catholicity can solve the problem which is so soon to confront us, and that Presbyterians need not fancy that the tide is to be kept out by excited protests or larger assertions of orthodoxy." Surely Dr. Morris is a John the Baptist, crying in the wilderness, "Prepare ye the way of the Lord and make his paths straight."

"I have heard," says Dr. T. D. Talmage, "scores of sermons explanatory of God's decrees, but came away more perplexed than when I went. The only result of such discussions is a great fog." If the fog is so dense that not a single glimpse of truth can flicker its way through, we might easily infer that sacred truth had no hiding-place in that realm. "Theologians sit on the beach," says Talmage, "and see a vessel going to pieces in the offing, and instead of getting into a boat and pulling away for the wreck they sit discussing the different styles of oarlocks. They keep on discussing the Divine decrees when there are millions of souls who need to have the truth put straight at them, that unless they repent they will all be damned." Such facts constantly multiplying among Calvinistically-taught thinkers demonstrate the necessity of new views in theology and marked advances for the Church.

Many Calvinists begin the construction of their theology by boldly assuming that absolute prescience is essential to the perfection of omniscience; but with absolute prescience, contingencies are, they think, incompatible. Contingencies being incompatible with absolute prescience, they must be outlawed. Contingencies being outlawed, every event from all eternity to all eternity must be fore-ordained. But the Calvinian assumption that prescience is essential to the perfection of omniscience is untrue. Absolute prescience of the free choice of accountable beings we have shown would be a momentous imperfection in the Deity. Let the Calvinist abandon this undue assumption, this fallacy prolific of so much ruin, and with its surrender the whole system of fore-ordination will fall. The news of such a fall would greet the angels, I think, with ineffable delight. "Many of the most zealous promoters of Universalism were Calvinistic," says Dr. D. Curry. "The reaction of Calvinism reached its development in Unitarianism," says Dr. Whedon. John Foster was a stern, ultra-Calvinist, and Calvinism almost unhinged his mind and made him melancholy.

The Arminian begins his construction of the system of theology by gathering facts, and from facts, rising to general principles. From his facts he infers that absolute prescience is essential to the perfection of omniscience. But between his facts and his conclusions there is no logical connection. No logician has ever been able to reconcile future contingencies with absolute prescience. The logical chasm between them the Arminian vainly tries to bridge over with a mystery. In the name of sound logic and common sense let the Arminian abandon a conclusion for which he has not the semblance of a reason, and which necessitates innumerable perplexities and contradictions; let him give up a system that is confessedly wanting in logical consistency. Most certainly Calvinists owe it to themselves to re-examine their reasons for holding opinions so generally rejected by the very wisest of men.

While there is much that is evangelical in Calvinism, "its most distinctive point," says George F. Wright, of Andover, in the "Bibliotheca" for 1880, "relates to the divine purposes." "There is," says he, "something truly sublime in the boldness with which the Calvinist faces the dark question of reprobation and attempts to reconcile this doctrine with the apparently antagonistic doctrines of the power, the wisdom, and the goodness of the Creator." Such devotion to John Calvin seems inexplicable. With all his many and great excellencies he was neither a model man, nor a perfect character. Canon Kingsley says, " He was a mystic, and a more conceited one, too, than even Henry Moore." Archbishop Laurence said, " His darling propensity was to systematize, and the predominant passion of his soul was his ambition to be a distinguished leader in reform. His prominence, however, was far from being acknowledged by his contemporaries, either in ability or in point of time." He was so truly an innovator in theology that Mosheim says, " He greatly prided himself in having departed from the notions generally entertained concerning the doctrine of predestination. He persecuted Castalio and drove Bolsec into exile for opposing his opinions on fore-ordination." Calvin himself wrote to Farel in his own handwriting, that " if his authority was of any avail, he would prevent Michael Servetus from returning alive." " I advised our magistrate," said he, " as having a right to restrain heretics by the sword, to seize upon and try that arch heretic, Michael Servetus; but after he was dead I said not one word about his execution." The injustice of this silence who can tell!

As the great want of his times, and also of those of the Dark Ages, was a lack of great modifying general principles, we can easily overlook inconsistencies and blemishes in the life and character of any one; but that a man with so serious defects, and with a doctrine so gloomy and shocking as to be acknowledged by its sincere believers to be "apparently antagonistic to the power, wisdom and goodness of God," should be so revered, canonized, and almost apotheosized, is a marvel in the history of theological opinion. I revere the name of John Wesley as much as any man of history. "Great," exclaimed Dr. Whedon, "were Wesley's logical powers; greater his administrative powers; but greatest of all his intuitive powers." But should Mr. Wesley teach me a doctrine so repugnant to the common instincts of humanity as unconditional reprobation, I should vehemently reject its acceptance. He did teach me the doctrine of absolute prescience of future contingencies, but I unhesitatingly repudiate it with acclaims loud and clear. Is it too much to ask the Calvinist to meet me in this theological compromise? "Would to God!" exclaimed Norman M'Leod, "that we could lose our Calvinism." (Page 357 of his life.) And is not Calvinism truly an unverifiable hypothesis? Is it not a worn-out system? New-school theology, with all its mighty efforts, only tried to hide the difficulties of Calvinism by congeries of subtleties. Light struggles with darkness before the day supersedes the night. The rising sun often dispels mists that dim for awhile its effulgence. Dr. D. Curry says: "The basis of old orthodoxy is immovable, but its superstructure is faulty and must be remodeled. A better psychology would speedily and forever finish this interminable controversy." "The majestic form of truth," says some one, "once walked the earth, but was dismembered and the sundered parts are wandering up and down in ceaseless, weary search each for the other, and each instinct with the old common life." The learned and venerated Sprecher, ex-President of Wittenberg College, says: "The fundamental tendency of the Reformation, its tendency to produce a clearer apprehension and a more complete appropriation of the Christian idea of the personality of God and of man, must eventually lead to the rejection of the doctrine of unconditional election, and of irresistible grace on the one hand, and of the block-and-stone theory of human passivity on the other. If man were a mere nature entity, the end of his being would be determined by his constitution; he would be purely passive under the operation of the force which supplied his wants and accomplished his destiny. But as he is a personal being, the end for which he exists is a goal, the attainment of which involves personal agency. The supply of his individual wants as a finite being involves free divine communication and free human reception; and his regeneration as a sinful creature, free divine operation and free human submission. It involves personal action on the part of God, and a personal action on the part of man. Though it must be regarded as merely a yielding act, still it is an act, that is, the subject of regeneration is not purely passive. The regenerating influence originates with God, but man yields to it. God produces the change; man accepts and acts it. God does not regenerate man without calling forth the action of the human will. The true Christian idea of God and man, as the experience of faith enables men more and more to apprehend it, will restrict the Augustinianism both of the Calvinistic predestinarian and of the strict Lutheran theories, and so modify the theory of Melanchthon as to free it from any unevangelical synergism." The ramparts of the melancholy doctrine of eternal decrees certainly must appear to be hideous to all profound thinkers. They are, indeed, sources of merriment to all unbiased by previous indoctrination. I submit it to a candid world, ought not this defenseless doctrine of election and reprobation to be publicly abandoned at once? The paths of evacuation from this fastness of Calvinism are macadamized with the rarest good sense and benevolence, and the sublimest of motives. The retreat of the great scholars, mighty thinkers, and hoary divines, from out this Genevan munition, would be greeted with hosannas, even from their own people, louder and gladder and more prolonged than those which fell upon the ears of our adorable Redeemer when he rode into the city of God. In the name of the perishing millions for whom Christ died, and who are patiently waiting for his law and his truth, let this unconditional surrender be made.

And, on the other hand, ought not the Arminian to abandon, at once, his not only needless, but troublesome, doctrine of absolute prescience? That doctrine is and always has been the great disturber of the peace through all the realms of Christian theology. But for it, light, joy, calmness and unanimity would be perpetual in the study of biblical truth. Not a single unfallacious consideration can be adduced that makes prescience a necessity. On the other hand, its assumption does necessitate innumerable perplexities. It surrenders free agency, makes a probationary state a farce, paralyzes the human will, exterminates all hope from the doomed, breaks the wholesome restraint of fear to all the elect and happily destined, mystifies all our thinkings, perplexes all our investigations, annihilates consistency from divine revelation, hampers all our efforts, renders every subject impervious to the light of reason, adjourns beyond the grave all settlement of fundamental theology, and furnishes perpetually masked batteries for the use of the logical Calvinians. It renders insoluble the great conflict between freedom and necessity, the conflict between the scientist and the theologian, the urgent questions which are now under discussion before the intellect of the nineteenth century. For if the future be now infallibly foreknown and certain and fixed, human reason protests against our moral liberty as vehemently as universal consciousness protests against the system of necessity. Admit prescience of future contingencies, and you necessitate an immobile fixity for the whole history of the human race, past and future, so certain in every iota as to obliviate all contingencies and make illusory the endowment of human freedom. But the assumption of the necessity of divine nescience of future contingencies is a hypothesis that works well in all systems and circumstances. I challenge a single instance in which it weakens or dims the force of any biblical truth, or breathes enervation into the energies of the probationer. Inertia makes astronomy the simplest of all the physical sciences. So divine nescience of future contingencies makes theology the simplest of all the intellectual sciences. Divine nescience is the new thought which solves every problem in Christianity that involves human reason, common sense and common humanity. It explains sin, freedom, election and foreknowledge. And besides all this, it leaves all the essentials of the Christian religion firm as Gibraltar. What more could be asked of any hypothesis? It makes our conceptions of the nature of God neither dim nor distant. It makes our relations to God neither indefinite nor powerless. Assume this, and most of the theological differences that divide Christians will be swept out of existence and their irritating discussions hushed forever. Nothing but nescience can stem the fearful currents of infidelity. There are innumerable intuitive truths which the human mind has never yet discovered. That a body cannot change its state was unknown until Galileo. Now it is known to be an intuitive necessary truth. Such an *a priori* truth, divine nescience of future contingencies will soon be acknowledged to be. Until then the freedom of the human will can never be seen in all the brightness of its full-orbed glory.

God says: " Son of man, thou dwellest in the midst of a rebellious house which have eyes to see and they see not, they have ears to hear and they hear not, for they are a rebellious house. Therefore, son of man, prepare the stuff (or instruments) for removing, and remove by day in their sight, and thou shalt remove from thy place to another place in their sight. It may be they will consider though they be a rebellious house."

Whether his people would consider or not was a pure contingency, and of this contingency he was not certain. Had he been he could not have said, "It may be they will consider." His language expresses doubt; and if he was certain his people would not consider then his language would not express the state of his mind, but made a false representation. Jesus, too, expressed the present uncertainty of future human volitions when he said, "I will send my beloved son. It *may be* they will reverence him."

Let us then assume just what God himself assumes, his nescience of future contingencies, and that in the kingdom of Providence he uses man as an instrument, while in the kingdom of grace he treats him as a person; and that as an instrument his will acts consentingly under the law of constraint, and as a person his will acts willingly under the law of liberty. By so doing every contradiction in the word of God, every absurdity in theology, and every tantalizing perplexity in Christian life and experience, at once disappear as night and its misshapen specters, when glad morning opens the gates of day. Not distinguishing between man as an instrument and man as an agent, led Locke and Reid and many others into bewildering and endless confusions.

The woes of theologians are the necessary sequiturs of undue assumptions. They have ever thought that they must chain God to some inflexible, inexorable plan, or the heavens would fall. But if their plans for God shroud every subject in absurdity and perplexity and bathe every energy in a upas atmosphere, they would better repudiate them and accept a plan vastly superior awaiting their adoption. For the only reasonable conception of this great subject is that of an ever-varying volitionating on the part of a free volitionating Ruler toward an ever-varying volitionating on the part of a world of subjects, free, rewardable or punishable in accordance with their free determinations. God depends, and must needs depend, on us every moment for what he can do for us. For if man is not free, human accountability is an idle dream. If he be accountable he must possess the power of pure self-originating forces.*

If man is free, his Maker is free. If God is free, contingencies are inevitable and logically necessary. Any general plan of pre-arrangement which extends to free volitions, put forth under the law of liberty and the power of alternate choices, is not only an impossibility in the nature of things, but it is a tantalizing absurdity.

Assume for Deity a plan appropriate to and in harmony with future uncertainties as to the determinations of free agents, and the Bible becomes the most harmonious book in the world, and all ortho-

---

* If man can originate sin, it must be by the exercise of a power, the *exercise* of which (not the existence of which, but the *exercise* of which) is absolutely independent of Deity.

dox evangelical Christians one harmonious household among themselves, and one harmonious army in the world, battling in different grand divisions the wily and malignant foes of our common humanity; not, however, fighting each other, but all fighting "the good fight of faith, and warring a good warfare." Sectarianism cannot endure the intelligence, liberality, refinement, urbanity and earnest work of earnest Christians. Sectarianism is not denominationalism. Sectarianism is devotion to a Church actuated by a selfish party spirit. Denominationalism is devotion to a Church actuated by the universal spirit of gospel missions. We, therefore, repeat that divine nescience of future contingencies is a necessity to the harmonizing of the two great bodies of Christian workers upon whom have come the ends of the world. In this view it is an indispensable necessity for the speedy success of the Christian religion. It is the thought so long missed and so much desiderated in theology, in theodicy, in Christian doctrines and in sacred exegesis. In our attempts at exegesis, we have often had too much of eisegesis.

I know the view I here devoutly advocate is not only radical, but it is revolutionary. But I humbly affirm that theology, not Wesleyan theology only, as A. A. Hodge says, but all theology and commentaries and exegesis, must necessarily be completely revolutionized in their basal facts and principles to meet the philosophical necessities of this age, and also to meet the varied and vast signification of divine revelation. If our theology would overcome infidel vandals and survive the twentieth century she must adhere to logic.

While clinging heartily to glorious mysteries, she must not advocate absurdities, and then remand them into the realm of the incomprehensible to be explained under the promise of a broader light in eternity. She must not ask superstition to relieve the Christian intellect of its legitimate work of logical processes, analytical discriminations and fearless enunciations. No light of eternity, however broad, can ever illuminate the absurdity that four multiplied by four equals seventeen, or that the sum of the angles of a triangle are equal to two right angles, or that freedom and predestination are terms not incompatible. We are sure to undermine faith whenever we stultify our reason as to the objects of our faith.

To theologians, mighty thinkers, philosophers, and philanthropists of all schools, whom I do profoundly revere, I make this devout appeal: Come, let us reason together; discriminating between absurdity and mystery, eliminating from our common Christianity all self-contradictions and as many imperfections as may be possible in the present state of psychology, biblical criticism, human development and personal religious experience. Certainly all must acknowledge that no set of men, even the wisest and best, could have formulated a system of religious beliefs that would never require revision, restatement or enlargement. All our orthodox theologies were formulated when the imperfections in psychology rendered impossible the conception of a consistent, comprehensive system of divinity.

"Truth," said Lord Bacon, "is not the daughter of authority, she is the daughter of time." "I believe," thundered Martin Luther, "that it is impossible for the Church to be reformed without completely eradicating canons, decretals, scholastic theology, philosophy and logic as they are now received and taught, and in their place instituting others."

"We bow," says Albert Barnes, "before no opinion because it is ancient. In all the momentous questions pertaining to morals, politics, science and religion we are greatly in advance of the past. Our hearts expand with joy at the prospect of a still greater simplicity and clearness in the statement and defense of the cardinal doctrines of the Reformation. Most of the monuments of past wisdom are capable of improvement in these respects. Thus we regard the works of Luther, Calvin, Beza and Owen. We look on them as vast repositories of learning, piety and genius; and yet we feel that in some things their views were darkened by the habits of thinking of a less enlightened age than this, and that their philosophy was often wrong. Had modern ways of thinking been applied to their works, had the results of a deeper investigation into the laws of mind and the principles of biblical criticism been in their possession, their works would have been the most perfect records of human wisdom the world contains. The subject of moral government is now better understood. A perceptible advance has been made in the knowledge of the laws of mind, and light has been thrown upon the doctrines of theology."*

"The body of dogmas," says Dr. Shedd, "was by no means fully apprehended by the ecclesiastical mind in the outset. Its scientific and systematic comprehension is a gradual process; the fuller creed bursts out of the narrower, the expanded treatise swells forth, growth-like, from the more slender. The work of each generation of the Church joins on upon that of the preceding." Dr. Samuel Sprecher says: "In this age of the dissolution of doctrine there should be made an effort to apprehend anew and to appropriate more fully than they could ever before be conceived and expressed, the results of the operation of the evangelical spirit in the past." "For creed," says he, "is the subjective apprehension of the infallible and unchangeable truth contained in the Scriptures. Creeds, therefore, being fallible and changeable, each generation in the course of the development of the Church should bear a part in the witnessing of those who compose confessions at particular times." Dr. Rainey, in the Pan-Presbyterian Council, said: "We are passing through a period of unexampled unsettlement of opinions. Every theological position is boldly questioned. Doctrines which have been accepted in all the great theologies have been thoroughly sifted." In the same Council Dr. C. A. Briggs said, "Progress and restatement are essential to the life of theology." "The present generation is passing from under the restraint of religious be-

* See note at the end of this chapter.

lief," said Dr. Hill, ex-President of Harvard University. Professor Van Oosterzee, the distinguished evangelical teacher in Holland, said recently: "A wave of infidelity is steadily advancing over Protestant Europe which the most favored country will not be able to escape. They have had it in Germany, we are now having it in Holland, and Scotland is beginning to feel it. In twenty years the Scottish Church will have it to the full, and all their orthodox theology will not save them." Dr. Campbell, of Boston, said very recently: "Moral power in New England is on the decline. The pendulum of religious belief has swung away from the orthodoxy of Puritan times. It has already passed its center, and is on its way to heartless nihilism." The Earl of Shaftesbury said a few months since: "Dark is our religious horizon; the hearts and minds of men are little suited to the exigencies of the times. The great danger of England lies, not in the activity of those opposed to religion generally, but to the vast indifference and apathy shown by the great masses of the people." The united faculty of Andover Seminary recently exclaimed in a manifesto: "If Andover Seminary is anchored to a special phase of orthodoxy in the past it might as well be scuttled at once. The path of New England theology is strewn with concessions to the truth and to an advancing knowledge of God's word. Genius will not be the slave of tradition, and it cannot stop the progress of thought." Such testimonies indicate that it is neither a crime nor occasion for malignity to inquire whether the formulated and received creeds are consistent with the present developments of mind, of knowledge and of religious life.

It must be remembered, too, that for centuries the Church was smoldering under the weight of the ashes of paganism precipitated upon it by Constantine. And while the energy of its living fires could not be repressed, its gleams could not be expected to be in pure brilliance, but wearing rather the lurid aspect of St. Augustine's Dark-Age teachings.

The Sensibilities, as a distinct department of mental philosophy, is only of recent origin. But some one might say, "If divine nescience be true, then theologians for the last nineteen hundred years have been wrong." To many this fact seems so inexplicable as to render divine nescience wholly incredible. But such must remember that the psychological distinction between the will and the sensibilities is not yet a hundred years old. "The trichotomy of the mental powers," says Sir William Hamilton, "was established by Emanuel Kant." Most explicitly did he refer the sensibilities to a particular and distinct faculty of the mind. For the want of this discrimination such works as those of Jonathan Edwards swarm with fundamental errors and false doctrines, his own devotees being umpires in the case. He says, "The affections are not to be distinguished from the will, as though they were two faculties of the soul." He makes an act of the mind identical with an impression made upon the mind. He says that "liberty is compatible with necessity," that "moral necessity is as absolute as natural necessity," and that " virtue does not consist in its cause, but in its nature." He advocates a kind of moral liberty which the penetrating Leibnitz pronounced to be just no liberty at all, but merely " elbow-room." He thus lays the foundations of his system in the quicksands of manifest self-contradictions.

Before this distinction in the mental powers, separating the will from the susceptibilities, was made, it was impossible even for the most gifted and learned theologians philosophically to construct a sound theology. For so long as the will is regarded as a sensibility it must be conceived of as acting under the law of constraint. Edwardean liberty consists in the external opportunity which a necessitated volition has to necessitate its effect. But if the human will be constrained, human liberty and systematic theology are necessarily rendered impossible. Consequently, for a hundred years Calvinism has varied its phases, but only with ever-increasing inconsistencies. Sometimes predestination is put in the sovereign will of God, sometimes in a limited atonement, sometimes in the limitations of the influence of the Holy Ghost, and oftener in the angle at which you look at the troublesome central horror. How untrue is the boast of Dr. Grier, editor of " The Presbyterian," that Presbyterianism is planted upon a munition of rocks older than Gibraltar! Episcopius, the pupil of James Arminius, pronounced unconditional election and reprobation to be simply an " upstart." There is no such thing as moderate Calvinism; it must be received or rejected as a whole. God either did predestinate from all eternity some of the human family to eternal perdition, or he did not. If he did, it can never be harmonized with immutable rectitude. It seems to me that the greatest of all the evils to Christianity are the clogs which predestination necessitates upon it. Surely God will not charge me with irreverence for rejecting contradictory propositions. For the last hundred years—since this psychological discovery, the trichotomy of the mind, was made—the dread *odium theologicum* has ever lifted its frowning menaces upon all those who were capable of sustained thought, accurate discrimination and logical processes, if they tremblingly ventured to advance outside of dominant creeds, however false and dangerous those creeds manifestly might be. "Nothing," says Dr. J. W. Alexander, "requires more courage and independence than to rise decidedly even a little above the par of the religious world around us. The way we commonly go on is not the self-denial taught in the New Testament." It requires courage to make advances in any thing. He who first spread an umbrella between his head and the pelting rain was hooted and stoned in the streets of London. Mike Fink, the untutored boatman on western waters, prior to the date of steamboats, studied so enthusiastically the expansive power of steam and the possibility of its application to navigation, that all considered his mind unbalanced. When he was dying he exclaimed, "Bury me on the banks of my beautiful Ohio, where the coming steam-propelled crafts may hail me as they pass." His conservative attendants exclaimed, " Poor fellow ! he is crazy yet."

He who exposes a popular absurdity or persistently advances a new idea, is generally suspected of weakness. The human heart opposes all kinds and degrees of progress. "It is common," said the brilliant Castelar, "to all reforms to excite great hatred, and the inheritance of all reformers is to have bitter enemies." Plato, after enumerating in the most admirable manner the traits requisite to a perfect human character, closes with the mournful confession, that should such a perfect being ever appear among men he would most certainly " be bound, scourged, tortured, blinded and finally hanged." And we have all read of a community which once begged that the greatest being and the most ardent friend that ever set foot upon their soil " should depart out of their coasts." Plato's description really seems like a prophecy of Him who spake as man never spake, and in whose lips and life there was no guile. " Should the Redeemer come again," exclaimed Faust, " the people would crucify him a second time." Millions, from their childhood, believe such absurdities as consubstantiation, transubstantiation, pantheism, the present certainty of a future uncertainty, the freedom of man while all his acts were sovereignly decreed from eternity, and the infallibility of his holy reverence the Pope of Rome.

But he who would sweep away any such refuges of lies is certain to be proclaimed as one who is harebrained, regardless of the revered past, blasphemous to Deity, a foe to the weal of the world, and must needs be burned or crucified. But after all denunciation and tergiversation, the world is full of poisonous trees shedding their baleful influences all over human society. It certainly must be the solemn duty of every philanthropist ruthlessly to hew down all such that may be in his power.

To me it seems that the affirmation of divine nescience of future contingencies gives a depth, reality, significance, simplicity and logical consistency to all the teachings of James Arminius which, as yet, they have never possessed. This assumption would constitute "a new Arminianism" that would be valid, logical, direct and inexpressibly inspiring. To force holiness into a free soul, or to make sin a blessed thing, is a self-contradiction no greater than to foreknow a future contingency. This eternal logic eternally thunders, and its reverberations are heard and felt all through the realms of theological thought and of thought systems. And he who affirms that he can see how the future acts of an innumerable number of free agents, through thousands of generations, all interdependent, acting and re-acting upon each other forever, can be systematized into an infallible plan, working out definite and designed results; and yet that those acts are absolutely free and thoroughly accountable, must always affirm it, and always does affirm it, with a hesitation of conviction and a quiver of heart which indicate a deep consciousness that there must be, after all, some latent fallacy in the mental process by which such a conclusion is reached.

I do not affirm that foreknowledge cancels freedom in a single specified case, but I do affirm that a foreknowledge of a future free choice is self-contradictory, because it is knowledge without any evidence thereof. All confess that prescience of future contingencies is a transcendent mystery which surpasses all the powers of the human understanding. "The freedom of man and the sovereignty of God can never be reconciled," said Descartes. I simply declare it to be not a mystery, but a flat self-contradiction.

DIVINE NESCIENCE A LIMITATION TO GOD.

I have long and prayerfully considered this subject, and it does not so appear to me. On the contrary, it clothes Jehovah, in my view, with ineffable glories. It necessitates to him power to create beings capable of performing acts which omniscience itself could not divine. It attributes to him wisdom, power and prescience sufficient, sovereignly, righteously and summarily to meet and manage all the unforeseen choices of uncounted millions. It secures to him, through all the realm of contingencies, a personal presence just as pervasive, efficient and immediate as he is confessed to have in all the realm of unintelligent nature. It ascribes to him a rightness so immutable, a justice so vigorous, a benevolence so peerless, a parental tenderness and watchfulness so unsearchable, that any excuse, explanation or vindication of his providence is entirely needless.

Nescience sweeps out of recognition and beyond power to harm, half the errors that have so bothered and crippled struggling inquirers, and so enervated our glorious Christianity. Without it the Bible is replete with perplexities; without it theology is a merriment to the superficial, and to the thoughtful it is a pugnacious derision. This doctrine not only enlarges our conceptions of Deity, but clothes man with unspeakable dignity. No other doctrine makes man appear more grand, accountability more certain, human freedom so wonderful, sin so hideous, eternal things so real and near, God so interesting to intelligent beings, or so interested himself in the vast possibilities and unforeseen developments of free beings created in his own divine likeness and image.

Many devout and thoughtful men hesitate at the necessity of divine nescience of future contingencies, inquiring whether it does not necessitate a pure adventure, on the part of Deity, in man's creation. But he could not possibly escape making man at a pure venture if he thought of endowing him with that quintessence of freedom which could render his accountability possible, reasonable or defensible. Accountability necessitates a plurality of possible actions. And if a being be endowed with a plurality of possible actions, each depending upon his own sovereign choice, selection and performance, without any thing anterior to that choice; then his creation could not have been any thing but a solemn venture on the part of Deity. And the solemnity of this venture the sacred narrative most clearly indicates. This is a necessity in the nature of things, which the Creator could neither remedy nor disregard in his creation of a responsible agent. A busy, earnest man has no time to waste on any body who asserts that God did actually realize his great purposes and glorious expectations in the case of Adam. If Adam's degenerated soul, and God's grief and lamentation over his creation, do not show that his making was a pure adventure on the part of his Creator, the human mind is incapacitated to appreciate proofs or to apprehend *a priori* truths. But seldom, indeed, in the history of the race has God realized his purposes and his expectations in reference to any single individual. How illustrious the divine plans and purposes relative to a distinguished American of the past generation must have been we are compelled to read in his varied and splendid endowments, his prosperous circumstances and his responsibilities as a statesman. Nature is proverbially parsimonious of her gifts to mortals, but she was most prodigal toward him, who was the pride of the land. She crowded capabilities into his mind, gifts and graces into his person, distinctions in his path, and clothed his tongue with the thunder and lightning of a vehement but classic oratory. But for it all how sadly was she disappointed and repaid! Her favorite son did nothing for liberty, statesmanship, civilization, education or science. He did nothing for reforms, missions, benevolent enterprises, and nothing for his country but to adjourn great pending issues, to be adjusted by a long, bloody, internecine war. He was not only destitute of moral force, but his life was wrecked, his motives were earthly and sensual, his soul was limited, his end was inglorious, and his memory is fast passing to extinction.

Now, who dare affirm that his creation was not a serious venture? If God sighed over Adam and regretted his creation, at the grave of the great senator he must have exclaimed, "O that thou hadst hearkened unto my commandments! O that thou hadst known in this thy day the things that belong to thy peace, but now they are hid from thine eyes!" God has very little in this world as he would like to have it. Every body and every holy cause more or less disappoints his reasonable expectations. He seldom finds a laborer in his vineyard he can implicitly trust. "For all seek their own, not the things which are Jesus Christ's." Every one knows that in himself God's reasonable expectations have not been realized; and if all have this conviction, there must be a basis for this universal consciousness. If God has not been disappointed, universal consciousness is false and unworthy of credence. If consciousness be unreliable, the investigation of philosophy and theology is the occupation of an egregious fool. But if God has been disappointed in his reasonable expectations, did he not create the world at a venture?

But how the Scriptures teem with evidences that this world was created at a solemn venture! "It grieved God at his heart that he had made man." "It repenteth me that I have set up Saul to be king, for he has not kept my commandments." "What could have been done more to my vineyard that I have not done in it? I fenced it, gathered out the stones thereof, planted it with the choicest vine. I built a tower in the midst of it, and also made a wine-press therein. Wherefore, when I looked that it should bring forth grapes, brought it forth wild grapes?"

These words express grief, disappointment, amazement and indignation. "Hear, O heavens, give ear, O earth. I have nourished and brought up children, and they have rebelled against me." "They vexed his Holy Spirit, therefore he was turned to be their enemy and fought against them." "When the Lord saw it, he abhorred them, and said, I will hide my face from them, and I will see what their end shall be, for they are children in whom is no faith." If these passages do not express contingency, uncertainty, adventure in the creation of man, we may despair of ever finding out the feelings of God or the meaning of his messages to a lost world.

NOTE.—E. De Pressensé says: "I conclude with a firmer persuasion than ever, that our effort must be to rise above the petty systems in which eternal truth is often held captive by the churches of our day, and to grasp it in its grand primeval type. It is only at such an altitude that religious faith and freedom of thought meet and coalesce."

CHAPTER XV.

THE REALITY OF TIME MAKES DIVINE NESCIENCE OF FUTURE CONTINGENCIES AN IMPERATIVE NECESSITY.

DR. BORDEN P. BOWNE, Professor of Philosophy in the Boston University, says, (see "Zion's Herald," March 6, 1879:) "We do not hesitate to call the doctrine of foreknowledge untenable, if it be assumed that time is real." Than this it would be difficult to find higher authority. The reality of time is, therefore, an exceedingly important question in the discussion.

Barnes, Emerson, Swedenborg, Drs. Haven, Hovey, Bowen, M'Cosh, and hosts on hosts declare that time is an objective reality.

Dr. L. P. Hickok says: "For place it was a prerequisite that there should have been space, and for period it was a prerequisite that there should have been time, and that both time and space be illimitable and immutable. Places and periods change in space and time, but make no changes of space and time. Time and space are concretes."

"Time," says Noah Porter, "is the ultimate reality which makes finite existence and activity either possible or even conceivable. It is the eternally possible ground of action and of creation." Julius Mueller says: "Time is an objective reality.

Every derived being requires time in order to the realization of its existence." "I can imagine that God does not exist, but I cannot imagine that time does not exist," says Joseph Cook. Victor Cousin says, "Can you conceive of an event happening except in some point of duration? Deny duration and you deny all the sciences that measure it. By denying duration you destroy all the natural beliefs upon which human life reposes." "I hold," says Sir William Hamilton, "that time and space are real conditions of things." "We cannot conceive of the non-existence of duration," says the wonderfully acute Samuel Clarke.

"Justice to Kant," says Dr. E. B. Andrews, Professor in Newton Theological Seminary, "requires it should be said that he does not intend in his discussions to take away, in the least degree, from the reality of time." "Kant," says Sir William Hamilton, "nowhere denies that time is a reality." "Kant," says Trendelenberg, "proved that time and space are subjective *a priori* conditions of perception and of experience. But he did not prove that they were only subjective conditions. He did not prove that they are not also objective realities." Vanpelt and others affirm that Kant really believed in the reality of time and space.

The angel who set one foot upon the sea and one upon the earth, and swore time should be no more, must have conceived of time as an objective reality. He knew that that event had a beforeness and an afterness which in some way must be distinguished in his conceptions. The reality which embraces that beforeness and afterness we call duration. An object existing necessarily suggests the space it occupies; and an object enduring necessarily suggests the duration it endures. The form of the object is addressed to the eye, the duration of the object is addressed to the reason. This conception of the duration of the object has an external occasion as truly as the perception of the object has an external origin.

Between 1800 and 1882 there is an interval of something. Between 1882 and 1990 there is another interval of the same something. The number of such intervals is endless. This something must embrace all intervals. But if this something embraces all intervals it must itself be beginningless and endless. If it be beginningless and endless it can embrace all epochs. This something is not a thing nor an object nor an agent nor a force nor an entity nor a principle nor a cause, nor can it act or be acted upon. It is the same whether events transpire or not. Successions of events suggest the necessity of this undefined something. Without the reality of this something there could be no succession of events. If no mind had ever existed and no event had ever occurred, this duration would have been just as much a reality. God might have made the world one thousand years before he did. Between that and creation did he not note the interval of duration? No illusion is possible as to the reality of beforeness and afterness. Hence, with that angel time was not a mere ideal subjectivity. Change necessitates duration, and things and the interaction of things cannot escape their relations to duration. God himself conceives of time as a reality; for at a definite point in it, he perfected the incarnation of his dear Son, and at another definite point in it, he accomplished the redemption of the human race.

Bishop E. O. Haven says: "As it regards the assumption of some that the categories of time and space are simply the imperfections of finite thought, and do not inhere in the divine intelligence and in the nature of things, I can only say that I do not believe it. I would as soon say that all the intuitions of the reason, such as right and wrong, are phantoms. If that is so, Hegel is right, existence and non-existence are the same thing. This affectation of supernal wisdom that emancipates the soul from the primary conditions of being is simply shutting the eyes, ceasing to think, and substituting an unborn dream for a clear conception."

Dr. M. Raymond says: "The non-existence of time and space is inconceivable. And when one says that they are mere subjectivities, mere conditions of being, to my thought he knows neither what he says nor what he means to say."

To all this overwhelming testimony as to the reality of time add that of universal consciousness. "In spontaneous thought," says Dr. Bowne, "time is the true condition of the world." Common consciousness never does question the reality of time, and the critical consciousness rarely has done so, and then only in the perplexities of recondite speculations. With such a weight of evidence, how is it possible for any inquirer to avoid the clearest conviction of the reality of time? "Making time," says one, "an independent being, sins against the law of reason, which forbids all plurality of principles." But time is not a principle. It can do absolutely nothing. It is a mere passive, independent reality, in the absence of which events would be impossible. "Time," says one, "is regarded as identical with eternity." Time is duration with a beginning and with an ending. Eternity is duration without a beginning and without an ending. All intervals of duration are embraced in eternal duration.

Dr. Bowne has, I think, written more profoundly than any other upon the time question. Much, however, of what he says would have been needless had it not been for the defenseless assumptions of those who believe in the reality of time. One may show the untruthfulness of the definitions men have given to time, and still fail to show the non-existence thereof. But by his wonderful acumen, penetration, grasp and comprehension, he emerges grandly, and wholly unfractured and unblemished, from the terrible fray. He silences, I think, forever, the ideal theory of time. No philosophic genius, henceforth, will ever venture to stand at its grave and bid it come forth again to annoy the republic of thinkers. The view he reaches is, he says, "a compromise between the realistic and idealistic theories of time." "Time," he says, "as an independent reality, is purely a product of our thinking. In this sense the world is not in time. But change is real, and change cannot be conceived without succession. In this sense the world process is in time. A being which is in full possession of itself, so that it does not come to itself successively, would not be in time. Such a being can be conceived as having a changeless knowledge and a changeless life. As such it would be without memory and without expectation, but would be in the absolute enjoyment of itself. For such a being the present alone would exist, and its *now* would be eternal. For those who can see the Infinite as such a being, the Infinite must have a strictly non-temporal existence. All change in the Infinite, as thus conceived, would not be a succession of different states, but a ceaseless conservation of the same state. There would be neither past nor future, but an abiding present."

In my work on "Foreknowledge," page 259, I pointed out the important distinction of God's subjective life and his objective life. I said: "In God's subjective nature his consciousness may not be a process of becoming and of passing away. This view may be necessary to maintain his subjective absoluteness. But, then, God must have an objective life in the vast world of contingencies. And in that life there may be in his consciousness a becoming and a passing away without in the least affecting his subjective absoluteness. God's knowledge of his ideal of the world is not identical with his knowledge of the world as it is actually realized through the agency of free beings. This objective realization of the divine ideal through such agency, though it cannot modify the absolute being of God, must be regarded as a process of becoming, and hence must be an increase in the knowledge of God in regard to pure contingencies.

God's objective life, that is, his life, experience, interest and enjoyment, as they are projected into and modified by his created universe, must necessarily be contingent. In his subjective life there is no such thing as contingency, failure or disappointment. There every thing is, in every respect, absolutely perfect, and is just what God desires and intends. This subjective life, in all its completeness and blessedness; high, sacred, changeless, fathomless and eternal; is forever past finding out. Of the glories of his subjective life even archangels can gain but glimpses in their sublimest conceptions and most searching inquiries. Such the subjective life of the triune God has ever been, and such it will always remain. But his objective life is as contingent as the choices of accountable beings are contingent.

While God is contemplated exclusively in his subjective and necessary mode of existence, his relations to contingent events and the relations of contingent beings to him, must forever baffle elucidation. If there be a contingent universe, it can be explicable and comprehensible only in the contingent relations which the Creator sustains to it. The overlooking this truth, and the consequent failure to distinguish necessities in the divine life from contingencies therein, occasions many and grave errors.

As God's objective life, that is, his life in contingent objectivity, must necessarily be contingent, therefore to rob him of the world of contingency is to rob him of that ever-changing interest, care, effort and benevolence, which a constantly expanding universe requires, and also of that ineffable enjoyment which an ever-varied contingency necessitates in the successive life of Father, Son, and Holy Ghost. It is this constant binding up of necessities with contingencies that forms the great source of confusion in theology and philosophy. How much wiser, therefore, would it be to keep these incompatible things separate and distinct in all our contemplations of God? This distinction between the subjective and objective existence of Deity can never fail to illumine the closet with a steady light; to invigorate, in every devout worshiper, faith in the fatherhood of God; in his special providence; his watchful loving care; and the reasonableness and deep significance of prayer, as one of the great controlling forces of the moral universe."

Dr. Dorner, in his recently-published work on "Christian Doctrine," in like manner sustains my views of the subjective and objective life of God. He says: "Absolute Being is not subject to succession, because he is steadfast in the flux of all temporal things. God in his internal being is exalted above time, above the succession of moments, above temporal developments, by his eternal absoluteness. This eternal self-containment of the absolute Being in his internal eternity is the pre-supposition and basis for both the negative and positive statements as to the relation of God to time and space. In the divine independence of time and space there is already a union signified of the self-containment of God and his altruistic containment of transcendence and of immanence. From his internal absoluteness, which elevates his being above extension and succession, God cannot decline. But if he cause a world to exist it is a logical necessity that he have a positive relation to time and space. His relation to time and history must be a various relation if there be a progressive world. God cannot have an eternally similar relation to past, present, and future time. If to him longer and shorter durations are equivalent; if relative to him one thing is not past and another present and another future, but every thing collapses into one point of the present, then history is a mere semblance devoid of results. God works in harmony with his world idea, in which is eternally involved what is new in a temporal aspect, but which is by no means so realized temporally that creative causality exhausted itself in the first act. He wills every thing in its season. Were God free from time and raised above time, he really would not be free. He possesses not only a transcendent existence in himself, but a transitive existence, an immanence in the world. He lives not merely an eternal life of love in himself, but a temporal becoming of his self-communication takes place. And thus his life of love in the world is subject to historical progress. With him there must be a difference between what is now past and what is present, and between the present and the future. God can no more regard the past of a converted sinner as present than he can look upon the future of the unconverted man as present. If, according to Augustine, God sees the past and the future as present, he would not see them as they are, and therefore he would not see them truthfully. There must be movement in the divine knowledge in order that it be true knowledge. This is so, because there is movement in things. God's interventions in time are conditioned by the nature of those things which the creature causalities have evoked. There are things which are not the effects of the divine will. Divine knowledge accompanies step by step advancing time and the developments taking place therein. And God's effective volitions have the same progress. There is a mutation in the divine consciousness, and this mutation is reflected into the divine will. Time, therefore, can be no mere subjective notion."

Thus the great Dorner sustains my view of the subjective and objective lives of God. And Dr. Bowne in his recently-issued "Metaphysics" takes the same ground. He says: "It is only in the self-centered personality that we transcend the conditions of time. But God is not merely the absolute person; he is the founder and conductor of the world-process. This last brings God into a new relation to time. This process is a changing process, and hence it is in time. The activity of God, therefore, in the process is essentially a temporal one, and God himself is in time so far as the process is concerned. As he is the chief agent in the process, and is incessantly adjusting his activity to the several stages of the process, both his activity and his knowledge of the advancing reality must be in time. A changeless knowledge of an ideal is possible, but a changeless knowledge of a changing thing is a contradiction. So knowledge of reality at any moment must embrace reality as it is; and if in the next moment reality has changed, the knowledge must change to correspond. The infinite, therefore, must be in time so far as the world-process is concerned, as this involves sequence in both action and knowledge."

Thus we see that one who, Joseph Cook informed me, is "the most distinguished metaphysician in New England," one who, Dr. D. Curry says, " is one of the greatest metaphysicians in this or any age," one whom the great Tholuck pronounced to be "the greatest mind ever given to Germany by America," reaches my identical conclusion, that with God, in his objective life, there are succession and time. Time, therefore, is a reality.

And if we must admit the reality of time, Dr. Bowne, a mind richly endowed for theological speculations, pronounces absolute prescience to be utterly "untenable." He perceived that the assumption of the reality of time logically necessitated divine nescience of contingent futuritions. And to conserve his early convictions, upon divine foreknowledge, he sought for proofs of the *unreality* of time, in the fathomless depths of Deity. In those depths he did perceive that the absolute One, in his absoluteness, could never be linked to either time or space. And from this he hastily inferred that time could not be a reality. But in his subsequent meditations upon God, in his objective, contingent state and life, he was compelled to affirm the reality of time, in order to escape many manifest absurdities.

If we do not study God through the human soul, how can we ever know him? And if we do study him in his relations to objectivities and to free-accountable causalities, through logical mental processes, we can never avoid limiting him by the absolute necessities of succession in events and duration as their measure. If the necessary laws of thought are not binding upon God, we can never know any thing satisfactory of him. All we can ever know is the necessary existence of a vast unknown, inscrutable, portentous power, of which we must stand in perpetual dread and awful apprehension.

Deny the reality of time; chain me in a durationless eternal now; rob God of all change; congeal him into the iceberg of indifference which prescience necessitates; prohibit him from changing in his feelings toward me, when from obduracy I turn and break in penitence at his feet; forbid him sympathizing with me in the perplexities of my way, and in the tragedies of my probation; and deny to him the interest, sympathy, and tenderness which alone can be born from a future unfixed and uncertain both for him and for me; and you fill my Bible with obscurity, my theology with paralyzing doubts, and you wrap in distressing gloom the glorious cross of Jesus Christ.

CHAPTER XVI.

CONCLUDING OBSERVATIONS.

WITH candor, but in vain, I have written to distinguished men for their objections to the views I advocate; I can learn from no one a solitary objection that possesses the least weight. Indeed, the very few objections to my theory which have reached me from various classes and ranks, clerical and learned, are so forceless, that my great respect for their authors compels me to suppress their names. The many-sided, penetrating Whedon writes me: "I have never made any objections to your view. I do not think it involves any grave heresy in those who think they can best explain the theodicy without absolute prescience. The notice of your book, 'The Foreknowledge of God,' by G. H., in the Quarterly Review, I yielded to admit very reluctantly, because I could not indorse it. I am, indeed, amazed at the intensity with which some persons oppose the view you entertain."

Bishop R. S. Foster writes: "Your book on 'The Foreknowledge of God,' though bravely taking issue with the view commonly held by theologians, and common Christians as well, I consider a most important and valuable contribution to the literature of theological speculation. It is able in the best sense of the word. It treats a most obscure doctrine with manly strength, candor and judicial calmness. Its temper is Christian throughout. It has the rare merit of presenting an old subject in a substantially new light. Its reasoning is clear and strong. The cause of truth needs the view it so ably presents. All thinkers owe you a debt of admiration and of gratitude for the manner in which you have done your work. I do not believe that the subject has ever been so thoroughly put or can be improved. And you have not transcended the limits of legitimate criticism and prudent dissent."

Bishop E. O. Haven wrote: "I confess when I inquire what I mean by freedom and foreknowledge, I find it impossible to conceive that the actual knowledge of which of two or more possible choices a free agent will make, does really belong to omniscience. I am glad that you and I can meditate on these themes without weakening our faith or diminishing our zeal. We have a right to think and to express our thoughts. Thus only can man do the work God requires of him. I thank you for your book. It is a credit to yourself, to the Church, and to the country. I hope the Lord will enable you to do much more work of a similar kind before you are called to the higher world."

John W. Andrews, Esq., of Columbus, Ohio, a gentleman who exerts as much influence in the General Conventions of the Protestant Episcopal Church as any layman in the nation, writes: "I agree with you fully in your proposition that what a free agent may choose to do cannot be a matter of prescience. We are forced to this conclusion by a logical necessity, which must be our guide aside from divine revelation."

Charlton T. Lewis writes: "Your book is the only one that fairly presents the problem it attempts. It is worthy of far closer and more earnest attention than it has yet received. It attacks and destroys the most prominent absurdity of the current hypothesis, and it prepares the way for a return to scriptural views of theology. The inattention of Methodist writers to your work indicates that they are far from awake to the real tendencies of contemporary thought toward scientific Atheism."

Some of the admirers of Dr. Dorner would still fain claim him as among the prescientists. True, there may be in the great and good man's mind some little hesitation, but certainly not vacillation sufficient to destroy my belief in his latent conviction of the necessity of divine nescience of future contingencies. I find in his discussions no pronunciamiento in favor of prescience or "against my view." But in his final summing up he does say: "Since God eternally knows all that is possible, future free acts are not to be excluded *in every case* from the divine prescience. At any rate God comprehends them as what is possible, since only the possible can become real. He knows in all circumstances his own acts proportionally to the act of the creature, however it may fall out. But whether there is in God a prescience of what free acts will really come to pass or only a privity to those acts when realized, at any rate God does not become conscious of their actual being before they become present." Such statements may express a mind not wholly decided; but if it be true that he really believes in absolute prescience he must reject the manifest implications involved in his propositions, and repudiate the results of his own assumptions upon this subject. He may have been enthralled in his consideration of this question somewhat by his difficulty in explaining prophecy in the absence of prescience. This difficulty relative to prophecy I have satisfactorily explained in my work on the "Divine Foreknowledge." A serious mistake, too, of Rothe and Martensen perhaps confounded Dr. Dorner still more. Those great writers deny the prescience of contingencies, and yet affirm that "God's plan will, nevertheless, reach its full realization." But really it may be questioned whether God's perfect ideal was ever completely realized in any one of his free creatures. For human beings God has world-plans and plans for eternity, clear, definite and unspeakably interesting. The realization of any of his eternal plans for free beings can only depend upon their own freedom. If they fail to do their duty the divine plans relative to them must necessarily fail. God's glorious plans for Satan and his angels were definite as the Gospel, but, mournful to relate, they never were realized. In like manner all God's plans which depend upon the free choices of free beings may be utterly defeated. Relative to persistently disobedient agents God's purposes never can be realized. Can the workings out of a divinely conceived plan be certain when the beings whom it embraces are all contingent in their choices? Dr. Dorner says: "In a definitive formation of a world-plan comprehensive of concrete personalities, God does condition himself by a regard to the use of creaturely freedom. God's plan, so far as it relates to free action, does not originate exclusively in himself. In order to the formation of the concrete world-plan, such as it will actually become, such as it will be actually realized, the foreseen use of freedom in the concrete must be taken into the account as woof adopted into God's conceptions."

He therefore pronounces "the question as to the prescience of future contingencies to be the most difficult of all dogmatic problems." He states, with great force, the many difficulties in the way of believing in absolute prescience; but how God's plan could reach a perfect realization while he conditions himself by concrete creature personalities seemed to Dr. Dorner utterly inexplicable. But though omniscience cannot foresee whether John will obey or disobey, as that would involve contradiction, he does possess resources (and herein is his amazing greatness) perfectly sufficient to counteract all the evil influences of John's disobedience, and then to accomplish by other means and agencies all that he designed for John to accomplish in his moral universe. But his plan for John individually would be a complete failure should he disobey. And what is said of John may be affirmed of the human race individually considered. In such a procedure God might be able ultimately to fully realize his general world-plan in all its particulars. By this means the danger that this general plan might fail of realization, which danger freedom engenders and necessitates, might be wholly obviated. This aspect of the subject, I think, should have been presented by Rothe or Martensen. Had it been, it would have removed a great obstacle interfering with Dorner's visions of the truth.

Dr. Dorner most satisfactorily exposes the fallacies in the argument of Schleiermacher in favor of the divine foreknowledge of future contingencies. But in his reply to Rothe and Martensen, who deny that God can know beforehand that free acts will become actual until they become so, he is mystified by sophisms far more reprehensible. The position of Rothe and Martensen is that the will to create free agents logically and necessarily includes the divine will to limit God's knowledge and action from a love of freedom. "But this self-limitation of God," says Dr. Dorner, "is untenable. It is untenable because it implies that there is a tendency in God to do every thing himself alone, and to know every thing, even the world of freedom eternally equal. It also implies that God's self-limiting will would oppose this tendency. But that would lead to a dualism in God, and would be an admission of a diminution in God for the sake of the creation and preservation of the world." This statement is utterly inconsistent with innumerable declarations and teachings of Dr. Dorner. The affirmation that the position of Rothe and Martesen involves such implications needs only to be stated to necessitate its denial. How Dr. Dorner could make it, is utterly inexplicable. The affirmation amazes me more than any statements with which I have met in all literature. Every reader will unite with me in its prompt and fearless denial. And this is the only refutation he can give to the invulnerable proposition of Rothe and Martensen.

But Dr. Dorner presents that which he desiderates in order to the establishment of the doctrine of divine nescience of free acts. He says: "In order to establish the denial of prescience it would be necessary to show that divine knowledge does not claim to extend beforehand to free agents, possibly just as we might show that the divine thought does not claim to think illogically, or that the divine will is able logically to will the impossible. But this is not shown by Rothe or Martensen. It is also not proved that it would be unworthy of God to know beforehand the results of freedom." He desires the disbeliever in absolute prescience to show "that divine knowledge does not claim to extend beforehand to free agents." But where could such "a claim" be found? There is no such claim to be found in divine revelation. There is not there a solitary line that even hints at a knowledge of future free choices of free beings acting under the power of contrary choice, or acting as free agents responsible for their actions. On the other hand, divine revelation every-where, in every utterance, assumes that God does not infallibly foreknow what will be the choices of free agents.

And for this claim there certainly is no foundation in the universal religious consciousness. Its unfairness, unreasonableness, deleteriousness and utter inconceivability, painfully impress the meditations of the whole race. Dr. Dorner wishes the denier of prescience to show that " the divine foreknowledge does not claim to extend beforehand to free agents, just as we might show that the divine thought does not claim to think illogically." But I inquire, is it not illogical to think that a free cause can have a real effect before it has an actual existence? If a free act be foreknown it has a real effect before it has an actual existence. Is it not illogical to think that a pure future contingency can be a present infallible certainty? It is not illogical to think that an absolute origination can be preceded by an incipiency? Is it not illogical to think that a proposition must be true which has never been revealed, which is destitute of proof, which is in itself entirely inscrutable to the human mind, which is prolific of absurdities, and which is without any considerations requiring its admission? " Freedom," says Dr. Dorner, " is the possibility of arbitrariness." Is it not illogical to claim infallible prevision and prognosis of a mere uncalculatable chance arbitrariness?

" Prescience," says Dr. Dorner, " makes God's relation to the world a lifeless relation." But is it not illogical to think that he " in whom we live, move and have our being, and from whom cometh every good and perfect gift," sustains to this mundane system a relation that is devoid of life?

Dr. Dorner asks that it be shown "that divine knowledge does not claim to extend beforehand to free agents, just as might be shown that the divine will does not claim to will the impossible." There is a genuine distinction between willing and knowing; one is an act and free, the other is a state and caused. But God cannot open and shut a door at the same instant, nor can he make wrong right, for these involve self-contradictions, and are, therefore, impossible. But for God to know an absolute nonentity involves a contradiction equally manifest, and is, therefore, equally impossible.

But the doctor wishes some one to show him "that it would be unworthy of God to know beforehand the results of freedom." He who has perused the previous pages has seen that such knowledge would be infinitely unworthy of a God of infinite benevolence. Such foreknowledge would cover him with disgrace, misrepresent his immaculate moral character, extract all meaning from his holy word, render impossible a respectable theology, and make his divine administration an irritating farce. Is it not unworthy of God to rob an accountable being of all the inspirations to meet his obligations which the actual uncertainty of his future is certain powerfully to arouse within him? Is it not wholly unworthy of God to hate and loathe a poor probationer for eternity before he ever thought of offending his divine majesty? But, reader, do not these hunted, unobvious, but weightless objections of Dr. Dorner, demonstrate the absolute necessity of divine nescience of future contingencies?

But the painful incertitude of the great and good man is distressingly manifest in his final conclusions upon the subject. (See vol. i, page 336.) He says: "Since God knows all that is possible, future free acts are not to be excluded in *every case* from divine prescience. At any rate, God comprehends them as possible. Whether there is supposed in God a prescience of what free acts will really come to pass, or whether there is supposed in God only a privity to free acts when they are actually realized, God is not conscious of their actual being before they become present." Necessity is in intellect.

In philosophy and theology the human mind instinctively seeks after the principle of unity in variety. And Protestantism is seeking earnestly, at this time, some principle in which all the great doctrines of our holy religion can find substantial unity. Alexander Balman Bruce, a broad-hearted Calvinian, in his "Chief End of Revelation," lays great stress on those aspects of divine truth concerning which doctrinal controversy among true believers is ended forever. He says: "I look forward hopefully to the certain coming of an era of grace in which such unity around the essential doctrines of our religion shall be much more manifest, and in which our revelation of grace shall wend its way amid the acclaim of all true believers, to universal triumph. In all probability the Church has many long ages before it, and one may, doubtless, dream of the glory that is to accrue to God therein as those ages roll on, and muse on the conditions under which that glory is to be advanced. Among these, in the judgment of many earnest men, reconstruction of the Church on a new and wide basis must take place. The Church is now weak, and among the causes of her weakness are doubt, division and dogmatism. To renew her youth, and make a fresh start in a career of victory, she needs certainly concord and a simplified creed." The "Presbyterian Review" for January, 1882, says: "The scheme of thought which most fully harmonizes the doctrines of grace in a coherent, logical scheme, possesses *a priori* claims to be considered in greatest accordance with divine revelation." The doctrine of the divinity of our Lord has been urged as the central article of Christianity. Some would fain put forth the judicial element as the rallying center. Dr. Thornwell suggests that "the doctrine of justification by faith may be the much-desired principle of unification." Dr. Vanzandt strongly objects to this, on the ground that the covenant of works and the covenant of grace "are antithetical, and in many important particulars are dissimilar." He insists that "the everlasting covenant determining all the events of time by the eternal and sovereign decree, is the central principle that implies all the truths of religion, of law or of grace." And yet, in deep sorrow, he complains that this very doctrine "has been allowed to fall into general neglect by its believers, and also that it has been treated with unutterable scorn by large numbers of those high in stations and great in attainments." He who supposes that the Christian Church of the future will unite in the supralapsarian decrees, certainly has not thought sufficiently on the progress of psychology and the brilliant revelations of ever-improving exegesis.

It must be admitted, without controversy, that the corner-stone of theology and of hermeneutics has never yet been found. Every fundamental assumption for these sciences which has been presented to thinkers has necessitated for them innumerable unthinkables in the process of their subsequent systematic constructions. But surely a doctrinal corner-stone for Christianity must exist somewhere, by which the whole building can be fitly framed and held together. The great thought which is here so confidently advocated, that of divine nescience of future contingencies, I am persuaded will ultimately be found to be the principle of unity which stands visibly, forcibly and lovingly related to all other truths of divine revelation. The incognoscibility of future contingencies is the central principle which illumes all Scripture with the morning stars of consistency, reasonableness and inspiration. It illumes, becalms and unifies all theological truths. It expels from theology all irritating dogmas and absurdities. It gives to the student of divine mysteries the animation of a seraph. It disenchants Christianity of not one of its resplendent glories. Theological propositions which are made in its ineffable light, beyond their mere statements, require little or no subsequent argumentation. They all fall upon the ear as the voice of God. They win unhesitating assent from all. Every inquirer is sent on his way higher up the mountain of divine thoughts, with a cheerful spirit and an elastic step, and finds the clouds ever parting for his enchanted feet. And when the theology and the Scripture exegesis of Christendom have reached a fundamental unity, what mind less than the infinite can embrace its boundless benefits and blessings! The evils that have so long and so disgracefully de-energized our glorious Christianity and bewildered the devout with dismay, will then be arrested as with the grip and arm of a giant. Sectarianism, suspicion, detraction, depreciation, uncharity, interference with each other's God-appointed mission and work, the diabolical miasma of caste in religion, the narrowness of socialism, the diversion and paralysis of Christian forces in moral reformations and in revival campaigns; all conspire to weaken the might, and delay the triumph of a holy evangelism, and to hinder the grand aims and realizations of the Gospel of the grace of God. By the operation of these baleful agencies immortal souls, to all human appearance, in uncounted millions, are endlessly ruined, and the glad day is deferred when "the knowledge of the Lord shall cover the earth, as the waters cover the mighty deep." Nescience cures all.

But what do I see when all Christendom agrees upon a corner-stone for the doctrines of Christianity which will necessitate no self-contradictions in our thinking, and no paralyses in our strivings to obey? I see a union of Christian effort in all the great world-reformations germane to the Church universal. I see a hearty co-operation of all Christians in the work of sound secular education, a work in every way inconceivable in its importance to the progress of humanity. I hear the voice of Christendom commanding the commerce of all marts, the amusements and literature of all educational centers. I hear it outlawing all customs corrupting to youth; branding with barbarism the nefarious traffic in intoxicants and narcotics; pronouncing the thunders of Mount Sinai in legislative halls, and along every judicial bench, around every electing precinct, and through every executive mansion; threatening all unfaithfulness to virtue, to truth, to principle and to unsullied patriotism with blasts more withering than those which swept from the earth the gathered host of Sennacherib. I see harmony reigning throughout all the branches of the true Church of Christ; each provoking all others to good works; all concentrating efforts in unselfish zeal wherever God is pouring out his Holy Spirit of awakening; uniting in sparse settlements and small villages those of different religious predilections into a single strong Church with a commanding minister at its head; co-operating in missionary operations in heathen climes, impressing profoundly the heathen world that Christianity has but one Lord, one faith, one baptism, one soul and one devout object — the present and eternal salvation of the human family. I see the watchmen seeing eye to eye. I see "the departure of the envy of Ephraim," "the cutting off of the adversaries of Judah." I see "the stick of Joseph and the stick of Judah becoming one in the hands of our God."

I see "the children of Judah and the children of Israel gathering together and appointing unto themselves a single head." I see "Judah no longer vexing Ephraim, and Ephraim no longer envying Judah." I see Jesus "setting up an ensign for the nations, assembling the outcasts of Israel, gathering the dispersed of Judah from the four corners of the earth, drawing the Gentiles to his standards, and to the brightness of his rising." I see him taking "the heathen for his inheritance and the uttermost parts of the earth for his possession." And with profoundest awe I behold him satisfied in seeing the travail of his soul, the promises being fulfilled, that "his rest shall be glorious." And I hear the angels, as the voice of many waters, singing, "Alleluia, alleluia, alleluia, the Lord God omnipotent reigneth."

Bishop A. Lee, diocesan Bishop of the State of Delaware, draws the following beautiful picture of the future Church of Jesus Christ:

"A bright vision has oft risen before my mind of a Church pure and primitive, combining the early organization, zeal and love, with the freshness, energy and progressiveness of the times; gathering from past ages experience, wisdom and liturgic treasures, while discarding utterly all corrupt additions and cleaning the temple from all profane intrusions; conservative without being narrow and bigoted; liberal without being lax; a true interpreter of holy writ, and yet referring all men, not to her own interpretation, but to the living oracles; rebuking with power worldliness and wickedness;

sympathizing with all that is good and heaven-born; a rallying-point for all who are weary of sectarian strife; a candlestick of the Lord, whose radiance should illumine our cities and forests, our mountains and plains. Is such an ideal never to be realized? Is it but a dream and cloud picture?"

Brothers, let us forget non-essentials, and pray devoutly for the realization of the Bishop's evangelical vision of the future city of God.

But as yet we know hardly the edges or the fringes of the blessed Bible. That book is a fathomless ocean of truth; and God, its infinite author, is a deep, infinitely more profound. Notwithstanding all that worthy scientists have done to increase invaluable knowledge, how little is yet known of the substances, qualities, forces, uses and histories of the multifarious objects of this insignificant globe! how interminable the discoveries in the realms of nature, awaiting the curious and the anxious eye of the naturalist! And yet vastly more discoveries remain to be made by devout students in the holy Scriptures, and also in the mind, the heart, the character, the plans, the procedures and the enterprises of the forever-incomprehensible Jehovah. As they contemplate the divine nature and are made partakers thereof, and watch the developments of the divine throne, they must inevitably comprehend more and more of the mysteries of their own nature, and more and more of the deeper and sublimer mysteries of Him "in whom we all live and move and have our being."

How can it be possible for a human soul to be

wise, calm, firm, discriminating, progressive, and always rejoicing among the beatitudes of which it is so susceptible, in the absence of devout and familiar contemplations of the infinite mind? And if it be thus profoundly engrossed in such loving and reverential meditations, how can it avoid making constant discoveries in those infinite heights and depths of thought, knowledge and sensibility which are forever to unfold to adoring minds, as they reverently stand before the august throne of the Eternal, or devoutly journey on and on through floods of light and fields of bliss in the contemplation of themes of unutterable magnificence and wonder, exclaiming, "O, the depth of the riches both of the wisdom and the knowledge of God!"

www.ingramcontent.com/pod-product-compliance
Lightning Source LLC
Chambersburg PA
CBHW022102230426
43672CB00008B/1252